CROSSING BORDERS
THROUGH
FOLKLORE

CROSSING BORDERS THROUGH FOLKLORE

African American Women's Fiction and Art

Alma Jean Billingslea-Brown

University of Missouri Press
COLUMBIA AND LONDON

University of Missouri Press, Columbia, Missouri 65201
Printed and bound in the United States of America

5 4 3 2 1   03 02 01 00 99

Library of Congress Cataloging-in-Publication Data

Billingslea-Brown, Alma Jean, 1946–
    Crossing borders through folklore : African American women's
fiction and art / Alma Jean Billingslea-Brown.
        p.   cm.
    Includes bibliographical references and index.
    ISBN 0-8262-1199-2 (alk. paper)
    1. American fiction—Afro-American authors—History and
criticism.   2. American fiction—Women authors—History and
criticism.   3. Literature and folklore—United States.   4. Women
and literature—United States.   5. Afro-Americans in literature.
6. Afro-American women artists.   7. Afro-Americans—Folklore.
8. Afro-American art.   9. Folklore in art.   I. Title.
PS374.N4B55   1998
813.009'9287—dc21   98-31339
                                                                           CIP

⊗™ This paper meets the requirements of the
American National Standard for Permanence of Paper
for Printed Library Materials, Z39.48, 1984.

Designer: Mindy Shouse
Typesetter: BOOKCOMP
Printer and binder: Thomson-Shore, Inc.
Typefaces: Gill Sans, Lithos, Palatino

in memoriam

KATHRYN NINA BROWN

June 7, 1975–April 29, 1993
I give her back to God with
gratitude, love, and admiration.

CONTENTS

ILLUSTRATIONS

Acknowledgments

From its inception, many people have contributed to this book. I am profoundly indebted to Richard A. Long, the Atticus Haygood Professor at Emory University, for his masterful guidance and mentoring throughout the years, for his devotion to a scholarship of integration, and for his generosity of spirit. I am indebted as well to Professor Chinosole from San Francisco State University, who read and responded to this work in very useful ways, and to Pamela Smorkaloff, who, through the Faculty Resource Network at New York University, provided valuable help in research. I am also grateful to Dr. Audrey F. Manley, President of Spelman College, and Dr. Etta Falconer, Provost, for their warm support.

There are a number of faculty colleagues at Spelman to whom I am indebted as well. With their foundational work on black women, Gloria Wade Gayles and Beverly Guy-Sheftall have been a sustaining inspiration for me. I have been helped in very particular ways by Gloria Wade Gayles, my "roomie," who has shared over the years her experience, commitment, intelligence, wit, and wisdom. Pushpa Parekh, likewise, has been a valued colleague, helping me early on to rethink and re-envision this work. I want to thank Paul K. Bryant Jackson, for his thoughtful reading of portions of the manuscript, and Mona Phillips, for her insistence that I give myself time to do the work. From the Department of Art at Spelman, I have benefited enormously from the collegiality of Arturo Lindsay, Lev Mills, and

Jontyle Robinson. I owe a special debt of gratitude, however, to Akua McDaniel, for so generously sharing her expertise. Those students enrolled in my seminar on border theory helped me in very special ways. For their hard work and insistent questioning, I thank Ayana Corbin, Kendra Gaskins, Nakia Brown-Threadgill, Melanie Harris, Maia Hunt, Nasya Laymon, Heather McGowan, Valerie Mitchell, Nova Smith, Sabrina Tann, Princess Tate, and Caroline Taylor.

I have deep and abiding gratitude for a communal network of friends who have listened patiently to my thoughts and who have always strengthened my understanding with a greater, more generous understanding of their own. Flora and John Mosley, Belle and Jim Harrison, Zina and Larry Stuckey, Ruth and George Lyons, Virgistine and Morro Sanyang, Mary and William Hester, Mary Casey, and Annabelle Kilgore are such friends. For technical support at critical times I am indebted to Irma Dixon and to Zeina Salaam and her husband, Nmutakala Jones.

I want to extend my gratitude and appreciation to the entire staff at the University of Missouri Press, but I am especially grateful to Beverly Jarrett, Jane Lago, and Julie Schroeder for their assistance and confidence.

Finally I thank my family, above all, my parents, Leila T. Billingslea and the late Harold Billingslea, who never wavered in their encouragement and faith. Morris and Janice Billingslea, Sandra and Richard Bowers, Tracy Bowers, Claudine and Efiom Ukoidemabia, and my paternal grandparents, Morris and Martha Billingslea, also helped to create a vital nucleus of family support that has sustained me over the years. David Thomas, my cousin and lifelong mentor, who read through the many, many drafts of this manuscript with persistent scrutiny and uncompromising honesty, deserves more than I can express here, but I thank you once again, David. Last, I thank my children's father, Kenneth E. Brown, and my children themselves, Stephanie and Christopher, who by their very existence keep me centered and eternally grateful.

CROSSING BORDERS
THROUGH
FOLKLORE

Introduction

For people of African descent in the Americas, forced migration, dislocation, and displacement produced an experiential borderland. Borderlands, Gloria Anzaldúa tells us, are present whenever different races occupy the same geographical space, whenever two or more cultures edge each other. Because borders are erected to separate, marginalize, and exclude, borderlands are sites of contestation, transition, and flux. At the same time, they are places of communication, negotiation, and exchange.[1]

In the United States, the shifting political and cultural landscape of the 1960s constituted a temporal and psychosocial borderland, a historic terrain where the lines delineating racial, social, and economic difference were challenged and exploited. For African Americans, the decade of the sixties was not only a time of intense political activism, but also a time of historical revision, shifting consciousness, and cultural affirmation.

This study takes as its point of departure the 1960s and the use of folklore as a strategy for border crossing in the works by two contemporary African American women writers, Paule Marshall and Toni Morrison, and two visual artists, Faith Ringgold and Betye Saar. It delineates how, during the 1970s and early 1980s, perhaps the most intense era since the Harlem Renaissance for the production and institutionalization of African American art, these women

I

manipulated material and expressive forms of folklore to transgress boundaries and devise an aesthetic.

Folklore, a symbolic construction informed by ideology, tradition, and the artfulness of everyday life, has been described by Zora Neale Hurston as "the boiled down juice of human living."[2] Historically it has resonated in the aesthetic sensibilities and cultural articulations of people of African descent in the Americas. Articulating the values, beliefs, and ethos sustained and re-created in diaspora, the African American folk matrix enabled displaced African people to establish differential identity, affirm group solidarity, resist dominance, and "recall home." The improvisational and hybrid forms of the blues, work songs, tales, jokes, and legends have since come to represent not only a category of knowledge and a mode of thought, but a kind of art. As an artistic process, African American folklore may be found in a number of communicative media. For that reason, black folkloric texts frequently cross into the domain of literature, the visual, and musical arts.[3]

In their creative and critical appropriation of black folklore, contemporary African American women writers and visual artists not only create art, but also construct alternative epistemologies. These alternative epistemologies, Patricia Hill Collins asserts, create independent self-definitions and self-valuations as well as articulate core themes. More important, as forms of subjugated knowledge, they challenge the very process by which certain other epistemologies, those of dominant groups, are constructed and legitimated. As an alternative, dynamic, and open-ended process for constructing knowledge and truth, the African American folk idiom, along with the literature and art expropriated from it, historically has offered ways to question the content of what was claimed to be truth and to challenge, at the same time, the process of arriving at that truth.[4]

Using folklore as a strategy for border crossing enables these artists to draw attention to the periphery, the space from which they question forms of dominance and reverse meanings. In engaging archetypes and stereotypes like Aunt Jemima and Sambo, these women transgress social, cultural, and epistemological borders, but for the purpose of reclaiming and reconnecting. Individually and collectively, they negotiate, cross, and recross to engage sociopolitical realities, fashion new forms of knowledge, and generate dialogue and empathy. In the artists' literary and visual expressions, folklore functions to define an African American cultural identity, to reclaim a certain femaleness within that identity, and ultimately to affirm the black woman's role in human and cultural continuity.

In linking contemporary black women's fiction and visual arts with folklore as the nexus, this study offers a framework for mapping the aesthetic sensibilities of four representative black women artists—Betye Saar, Faith Ringgold, Toni Morrison, and Paule Marshall. To begin, I document the use of expressive forms of folklore, such as tales, legends, and songs, in Marshall's and Morrison's fiction and the use of material forms of folklore—quilts, dolls, and puppets, for example—in the visual art by Ringgold and Saar. Second I propose the conceptual paradigm of a "folk aesthetic"—an aesthetic of functional form, conjunctive duality,[5] and ironic signification—to designate the strategies by which these women transgress borders and locate sites of intervention. And it is from these sites that they articulate new dimensions of consciousness as they theorize and affirm identity.

Finally, I engage the ongoing work in cultural studies and feminist and black aesthetic theory to foreground multi- and interdisciplinarity, themselves forms of border crossing, as praxis. Because border theory, the metaphor of borderlands in particular, translates the phenomena of shifting, multiple, heterogeneous borders where different histories, experiences, perspectives, and voices intermingle,[6] I find it a useful construct to interrogate and frame black women's creative sensibilities as expressed across art forms in place and time.

My analysis of the fiction produced by Paule Marshall and Toni Morrison and visual art by Faith Ringgold and Betye Saar during the 1970s and early 1980s is based on several related assumptions. The first is that through diverse relations of power and privilege, the spheres of art and aesthetics produce knowledge and translate identity.[7] The second is that art is a historically and culturally specific phenomenon, reproducing not only the values, attitudes, and convictions of the artist, but history and culture as well. Finally I proceed from the assumption that there is no single sphere of human activity or historical period for which gender issues cannot be raised.

The first chapter, "Folklore and the Borderland of the Sixties," delineates how the political and sociocultural formations during the 1960s constituted a psychosocial and ideological borderland. In the context of integrationist and nationalist ideologies, I examine the emergence of certain critical and aesthetic formulations for African American art and discuss how these formulations both derived from and shaped attitudes about black folklore. I likewise clarify how engagement with stereotypical images constructed and derived from African American folk types was central to the formation of oppositional cultural practices and their expression in art.

The second chapter, "Folk Magic, Women, and Identity," interrogates the representation of folk magic—conjure, hoodoo, and voodoo—in Morrison's and Marshall's fiction and in Saar's and Ringgold's visual art. Considered during the 1960s to be a notable and distinct feature of black Atlantic culture, folk magic represented continuity with Africa and provided the needed spiritual reference for the formation of cultural identity. Definitively linked to black female subjectivity, folk magic in the works of these four women also represents a transgressive spiritual power, a power by which female experience is imbued with awe and reverence or "sacralized," and a power that is used to challenge ultimately the exclusionary practices of patriarchist black nationalism.

Chapter 3, "Reclaiming and Re-creating Africa: Folklore and the 'Return to the Source,'" identifies the ways in which the journey in Marshall's and Morrison's fiction, along with the use of symbols, materials, and techniques reflecting *Africanité* in Saar's and Ringgold's visual art, situates a metaphoric return to and an aesthetic re-creation of Africa. For African Americans, the return to and re-creation of Africa meant crossing geopolitical, cultural, and psychosocial borders for the purpose of reclaiming and reconnecting. Throughout the 1970s and into the 1980s, the reclamation and rediscovery of Africa in literary and visual expressions was central to the production of a functional, collective, cultural identity.

The fourth and final chapter, "Folklore as Performance and Communion," examines how the reproduction of the affective, participatory relationship between artist and spectator in "performance art" and the representation of rites of unitive presence and collectivity in fiction enable the activation of a "sense of communion" in the art by these four women. Moving beyond thematic definitions, this chapter proffers a secularized concept of communion, one that includes and transcends traditional Christian references to the sacraments. Contextualized and defined as a performative element from black folk culture, the sense of communion as evidenced in their work addresses the degree to which a work of art is equally constructed by the artist and the viewer. Activating and replicating a conjunctive duality, communion powerfully translates the intellectual, intuitive, and form-giving energies characterizing the aesthetic of these four women.

Betye Saar, Faith Ringgold, Toni Morrison, and Paule Marshall are contemporaries and still living. Continually negotiating, crossing, and recrossing the borders between the personal and the political, between racial, national, and social identities, each of these women has been and remains a border crosser. For Betye Saar, one of the first two black women to exhibit at the Whitney Museum of American Art, the crossing to the New York art world was enabled in part, and significantly, by Faith Ringgold's activism. Ringgold, a participant in a 1970 demonstration by the Ad Hoc Women's Art Group against the Whitney Museum's Sculpture Annual, agitated specifically for the inclusion of two black women. The consequence was Barbara Chase-Riboud and Betye Saar becoming the first two African American women to be included in a Whitney Sculpture Annual.

Saar, who gained national attention in 1969 with *Black Girl's Window*, was born July 30, 1926, in Los Angeles, where she was reared and presently lives. Academically trained with a B.A. from UCLA, Saar has been the recipient of two fellowships from the National Endowment for the Arts and has had solo exhibitions at the San Francisco Museum of Modern Art, the Quay Gallery, the Baum-Silverman Gallery, the Berkeley Art Center, the Museum of Contemporary Art in Los Angeles, and the California Afro-American Museum. In both group and solo exhibitions, Saar's work has been shown internationally, from South Africa to Australia, from Cuba to Canada, from Brazil to the Netherlands. Included in the collections at the National Museum of American Art, the Metropolitan Museum of Art, the Studio Museum in Harlem, the High Museum in Atlanta, and the San Francisco Museum of Contemporary Art, among others, her works have been the subject of several films and videos: *The*

Originals: Women in Art Series; Spiritcatcher: The Art of Betye Saar; Art is a Verb; and most recently, in collaboration with her daughter, *Betye and Alison Saar: Conjure Women of the Arts.*

Saar works principally in mixed-media collage and assemblage, which range from small enclosures and "boxes" to altars and site installations. Her works project a series of ideas, many of which during the late 1960s and the 1970s were clearly political in nature. Her thematic concerns include social and political commentary, various forms of the occult, and what she herself identifies as "a curiosity about the mystical."

Paule Marshall was born on April 9, 1929, in Brooklyn, New York. Her parents, Samuel and Ada Burke, were Barbadians who immigrated to the United States after the First World War. With a major in English, Marshall graduated Phi Beta Kappa from Brooklyn College in 1952 and published her first novel, *Brown Girl, Brownstones,* in 1959. A collection of short fiction, *Soul Clap Hands and Sing,* was published in 1961; then came *The Chosen Place, the Timeless People* in 1969, *Reena and Other Stories,* and *Praisesong for the Widow* in 1983, and *Daughters* in 1991.

Marshall's fiction reproduces the tensions between Afro-Caribbean and Euramerican culture, but in each of her works, she delineates characters, typically black women, as they are shaped by and as they transgress cultural traditions to reclaim some elusive aspect of identity. Pursuing narratively what Carole Boyce Davies has called "the traffic between multiple and various identities," Marshall's fiction has been described as representing movement toward wholeness and has been named a "literature of reconnection."[8]

A self-identified black feminist artist, Faith Ringgold was born October 8, 1930, in Harlem. With a B.A. and M.A. from City College of New York, she has been awarded two National Endowment for the Arts Fellowships, one for sculpture in 1978, and another for painting in 1980. She was also the recipient of a Guggenheim Memorial Foundation Fellowship in 1987, and the NEA Award for Painting in 1989. She has had numerous solo exhibitions, a twenty-year retrospective at the Studio Museum in Harlem in 1984, a major twenty-five-year survey in 1990 that traveled to thirteen museums nationwide, and, most recently, at the ACA Galleries in New York, she had a retrospective of works done over the last thirty-one years.

Ringgold's works in the 1960s were large stark canvases, depicting scenes with evident political and social content. In the early 1970s she began to explore different media, creating soft sculpture and what she calls "soft people." For the last several years, her principle medium has been painted and pieced fabric in the structural format of narrative quilts. Combining painting, stitchery, photo etching, and traditional folk narrative, Ringgold's quilts are included in a number of private and public collections, including the Metropolitan Museum of Art, the Guggenheim Museum, the High Museum, the Boston Museum of Fine Art, and the Museum of Modern Art. Ringgold has also been the subject of several films and videos, two of which are *Faith Ringgold: The Last Story Quilt* (1991) and *Faith Ringgold Paints Crown Heights* (1995). In 1996 Ringgold installed the *Crown Heights Children's History Story Quilt*, a quilt that depicts folktales from the twelve dominant cultures originally represented in Crown Heights.

Transgressing the boundaries between written and visual art, Faith Ringgold has also published quite extensively. Her publications include her memoirs, *We Flew over the Bridge: The Memoirs of Faith Ringgold* (1995), and several children's books, *Aunt Harriet's Underground Railroad in the Sky* (1992), *Dinner at Aunt Connie's* (1993), and, most recently, *My Dream of Martin Luther King* (1996).

Nobel Laureate Toni Morrison was born Chloe Anthony Wofford on February 18, 1931, in Lorain, Ohio. With a B.A. from Howard University and an M.A. from Cornell University, Morrison has been a senior editor at Random House and a professor at Texas Southern University, Howard University, Columbia University, and Yale University. Currently she holds the Robert Goheen Professorship in the Humanities Council at Princeton University. A recipient of the National Book Critics Circle Award, the Pulitzer Prize for Fiction, and the Chianti Ruffino Antico Fattore International Award in Literature, Toni Morrison has published seven critically acclaimed novels: *The Bluest Eye* (1970), *Sula* (1974), *Song of Solomon* (1977), *Tar Baby* (1981), *Beloved* (1987), *Jazz* (1992), and *Paradise* (1998). She has also written a musical, *New Orleans* (1983); a play, *Dreaming Emmett* (1986); and a collection of essays, *Playing in the Dark: Whiteness and the Literary Imagination* (1992). Using history, "enchantment," and folklore to translate African American diasporic culture, Toni

Morrison is a popular writer whose work nevertheless commands serious scholarly attention. Like Ringgold, Saar, and Marshall, Morrison's engagement with the material and expressive forms of folklore in her work make manifest the intellectual, intuitive, and form-giving energies informing her aesthetic. The engagement with folklore, for these artists, is a consequence of their response to the shifting consciousness of the 1960s cultural revolution.

1

FOLKLORE AND THE BORDERLAND OF THE SIXTIES

There was always a border beyond which the Negro could not go, whether musically or socially. . . . And it was this boundary, this no man's land, that provided the logic and beauty of his music.

LeRoi Jones (Amiri Baraka)

The border for us is an elastic metaphor that we can reposition in order to talk about many issues.

Guillermo Gómez-Peña

The decade of the sixties in the United States, marked by civil rights and black power, assassinations and urban riots, and radical student dissent and antiwar protests, was a threshold decade. It was a time of transition, flux, and struggle between ideologies, races, and generations. Related to what Victor Turner calls a "liminoid phenomenon," the 1960s was an interstitial, historic space, a locus of actual and potential transgression, and a "seedbed of cultural creativity." For African Americans, the decade was a political and sociocultural frontier, a border zone between the lived experience of social control and the dream of social justice. And like the geopolitical borderland, the geographical space where races, cultures, and languages edge each other, the sixties was a time when people negotiated and translated the meaning of identity.[1]

Theorizing identity, especially in the context of Africa and its diasporas, means addressing, as Paul Gilroy discerns, the tension between chosen identities and given identities. It also means addressing

9

issues of difference as well as the nature of subjectivity. While recent postmodernist theorizing resists or even dismisses notions of identity based on the concept of a unitary subject, some scholars have interpreted that resistance itself as a move to "destabilize potentially comforting communal identities." The scholar and theorist Nancy Hartsock, for instance, has called attention to the suspicious nature of such efforts to dissolve the subject:

> Somehow it seems highly suspicious that it is at this moment in history, when so many groups are engaged in "nationalisms" which involve redefinitions of the marginalized Others, that doubt arises in the academy about the nature of the "subject." . . . Why is it, exactly at the moment when so many of us who have been silenced begin to demand the right to name ourselves, to act as subjects rather than objects of history, that just then the concept of subjecthood becomes "problematic"?

In a similar vein, the literary critic and theorist Henry Louis Gates Jr., describing these efforts as the "critical version of the grandfather clause," has written, "Consider the irony: precisely when we (and other third world peoples) obtain the complex where-withal to define our black subjectivity in the republic of Western letters, our theoretical colleagues declare that there ain't no such thing as a subject. . . ."[2]

For African Americans, the conditions for the formation of a functional identity assumed urgent and collective overtones during the 1960s and were linked, not only to history and socioeconomic and political power, but also to the spheres of art and aesthetics. Definitions of identity, however, were problematized by the tensions between the civil rights and black power movements, both of which, ironically, had made a politics of identity possible. In transforming existing power relations to open new cultural spaces, these two movements enabled black Americans to define, perhaps for the first time since the 1920s, a functional, collective identity and to mobilize those definitions through the creation and control of cultural institutions. Conceived as a collective, true self reflecting shared codes and a common historical experience, cultural identity was thought to be a function of history, memory, and consciousness.[3]

The nature of that history and consciousness and the origin and source of cultural memory marked, however, another arena of contestation. Because the civil rights movement was closely linked to a southern-based folk heritage, the African American folk tradition was associated with that movement and considered by many to be a source for derogatory images and stereotypes. At the same time, folklore was recognized as the site of cultural memory and a vast repository for creative expression. It was therefore positioned at that interstitial space where the borders framing identity, continuity, and art were crisscrossed, ruptured, and reframed. And for that reason, folklore during the sixties, especially in its connection to dominant modes of representation, was a contested terrain, one that was negotiated, translated, and transformed.

Then, too, although African American cultural identity, particularly in relation to art and other forms of representation, was constitutive of difference, it was difference around the coordinate of race. Identity politics during that decade, both nationalist and integrationist, was still male-dominated. There was little analysis of gender power and very little regard for the lack of congruence between the social and political aspirations of the racial group as a whole and the relative status of its female members.[4]

Nationalist ideology in particular promoted contradictory if not misogynist constructions of black womanhood that were insinuated into a number of diverse spheres of culture. Following the infamous report *The Negro Family: The Case for National Action*, published by Patrick Moynihan in 1965, black nationalist discourse identified black women as active agents in the economic and social emasculation of black men.[5] There was likewise the uncritical acceptance of the implication that restoring black men as heads of households would redress the effects of racism and remedy the supposed pathology of the female-headed black family. This position, however, equated the domain of domestic patriarchal privilege with racial equality and left unaddressed the very real claims of black women to racial and gender equality.[6]

Although they were located on the periphery of nationalist discourse, black women writers, artists, and intellectuals traversed the boundaries erected around the domains of history, identity, image, and art and produced works that interrogated and subjected nationalist discourse to critique, especially with regard to gender. The writer, intellectual, and activist Toni Cade Bambara was one of the first to launch these interrogations and expose the lack of congruence between nationalist aspirations for social justice and self-determination and the position of women. Writing in her 1970 anthology, *The Black Woman*, Bambara first asserted that black women's "art, protest, dialogue no longer spring from the impulse to entertain, or to indulge, or to enlighten the conscience of the enemy; white people, whiteness, or racism; men, maleness, or chauvinism." She then went on to establish the preconditions for the emergence of gendered response to patriarchist nationalism: "If we women are to get basic, then surely the first job is to find out what liberation for ourselves means, what work it entails, what benefits it will yield."[7]

In her study of black women novelists and the nationalist aesthetic, Madhu Dubey theorizes that black women collectively interrogated, restructured, and supplemented the 1960s ideological program of black cultural nationalism and generated "a unique vision of identity, community, and historical change."[8] I submit further that to do so, they promoted and translated the emancipatory energies of a folk consciousness to the realm of art and aesthetics. Equally important, they implemented strategies to transform the material and expressive forms of folklore from sites of oppression to spaces of intervention and resistance.

THE MOVEMENT, JEMIMAS, AND MYSTICISM

In *The Liberation of Aunt Jemima* (1972) (Figure 1), *Imitation of Life* (1972) (Figure 2), *Black Crows in the White Section Only* (1972), and *All God's Chillun* (1976), California artist Betye Saar takes advantage of the strong visual imprint made by stereotypical images like Sambo and Aunt Jemima to create a series of works projecting nationalistic, "black liberation" themes.[9]

These works are empowered by the artist's use of mixed-media assemblage and collage placed in boxes. Through their formulation of subjects from multiple media, collage and assemblage invite disjunctures in meaning and embrace discontinuities and fragments.[10] The assemblage of folk stereotypes and memorabilia into visual representations of the African American cultural experience emphasizes the disjunctures and discontinuities of that experience as it critiques its distortions. Moreover, just as boxes frame, enclose, and delineate boundaries, these works encase the historical particularity of that

Figure 1. Betye Saar, *The Liberation of Aunt Jemima,* 1972. Mixed-media assemblage, 11¾" × 8" × 2½". Collection of the artist. Photo by Lezley Saar.

Figure 2. Betye Saar, *Imitation of Life*, 1975. Mixed-media assemblage, 7" × 4" × 3". Michael Rosenfeld and Halley K. Harrisburg.

experience, give it new meaning, and move it into the gallery. In that context, these works constitute a crossing, not only from black folk culture into the plastic and pictorial "high" arts, but also from past to present, from blighted history to new definitions of identity.

Saar charges her political statements by transforming and, in her own words, "recycling" stereotypical folk images. As she explains,

> During the late sixties, during the black revolution, [my] work became very political. I think that was my way of responding to what was happening in the United States and the treatment of Blacks in the South and also a reaction to the death of Martin Luther King. I had previously started to collect derogatory black images and I recycled them in my work.[11]

At a time when the art world was hostile to the expression of the personal, to visualizations of memory and place, Saar's recycling of these images transgressed boundaries and contested not only the meanings imposed on these images, but also the ideas in the contemporaneous art world about what was suitable for and who was capable of making art.

Just as Betye Saar uses visual language to engage the politics of representation, Paule Marshall uses the written word. Traversing cultural and geopolitical boundaries, Marshall transforms black Atlantic folk forms and the tradition of oral narrative performance into fiction. From the writer's own account, the late afternoon ritual of gossip and storytelling in the "wordshop" of her mother's kitchen, where Barbadian women "recounted endless tales of obeah . . . of conjure, roots, or mojo or vodun," was an important early influence on her work.

> I was impressed, without being able to define it, by the seemingly endless way they had mastered the form of story-telling. They didn't know it, nor did I at the time, but they were carrying on a tradition as ancient as Africa, centuries old oral mode by which culture and history, the wisdom of the race had been transmitted. . . . Their skill with language and the strong political cast to their talk . . . helped to shape me as a writer.[12]

Cognizant of what she calls the "peculiar kind of female folklore" created by these women, Marshall attempts, in her own words, to replicate their "ability to work magic with language."[13] As a consequence, folk ritual and the pattern of oral narrative performance inform the structure and content of *The Chosen Place, the Timeless People* (1969) and *Praisesong for the Widow* (1983). In these works, the characteristic openings and closings of the Caribbean folktale, the hesitations and repetitions of oral performance, along with references to runagate, lavé tête, and Africans walking on water, are specific elements of the black folk tradition Marshall employs to reach her "expressly political" themes: the quest for cultural identity and the journey back into the historical self.[14]

The journey across geopolitical, cultural, and ideological borders constitutes one of the most frequent crossings in black women's fiction. Interpreted at one point as the movement from "victimization to consciousness" and from "division to wholeness," the journey was perceived to be as much personal and psychological as political and social. Marshall, however, a veteran of the Harlem Writers Guild and participant in its 1960s cultural and social activism, insists on "the

essentially political perspective" in her art.[15] Thus, while the journey
in her fiction leads to self-knowledge, it does so because the protagonist transgresses boundaries and creates a space for intervention.
From that space, she engages the historical experience and shared
cultural codes to reproduce and rediscover identity.

Moving her female protagonists from points in the New World
like North White Plains, New York, to the Caribbean, and then
having them express intentions to visit Africa, Marshall consciously
orchestrates journeys across geographical space and time that, she
explains, are "meant to serve as a metaphor for the psychological
and spiritual return back over history which I am convinced Black
people in this part of the world must undertake." Enlarging her
statements of artistic intent to aesthetic imperative, the writer defines
the twofold task of the black writer. The first is "to make use of the
rich body of *folk* and historical material that is there," and the second
is to "interpret that past in heroic terms."[16] Redefining black history
and culture in both North American and Caribbean contexts, Paule
Marshall reclaims the black folk idiom as a strategy to resist cultural
dominance.

In Marshall's fiction, then, folk materials are consciously employed
for a "heroic interpretation" of the past. In the fiction of Toni Morrison, folklore is a device for reclamation and rediscovery of the
"ancestor," the "ancient properties," and the "village values" necessary for the survival and sustenance of community. While Morrison's
works focus on individual conflicts, triumphs, and failures, explor-
ing the remnants of the "spaces and places in which a single person
could enter and behave as an individual within the context of community,"[17] the salvation of the individual is not the point. Individuals
in Morrison's fiction define themselves both inside and outside communal boundaries, but ultimately it is the strength and continuity of
community and culture that are at stake and being tested.[18]

Conscious that her emphasis on community, on the vital presence
and love of the ancestor, has been too often confused with "some
simple-minded cant about Black families, broken families, or history-
lessness" and construed in critical circles as pejoratively "political,"
the writer asserts, "If anything I do, in the way of writing novels (or
whatever I write) isn't about the village or the community or about
you, then it's not about anything."[19]

The village and the notion of community, however, are problematized in Morrison's work. In her first two novels, *The Bluest Eye* (1970) and *Sula* (1974), individuals, especially girls and women, become scapegoats and pariahs because, as the writer explains, "The black community is a pariah community."[20] As a pariah itself, the community is unable to sustain its members because it is without the ancestor, the spiritual sage and advisor who would "defy the system, . . . provide alternate wisdom, and establish and maintain and sustain generations in a land." Embodying communal resources, the ancestor is valuable not only because she is wise, but because she values "racial connection and racial memory over individual fulfillment."[21]

In *Song of Solomon* (1977) and *Tar Baby* (1981), the problematics of community, cultural identity, and racial connections are explored and resolved through the use of folklore. In *Tar Baby*, Morrison synthesizes the African legend of the tar lady with its Caribbean and southern American variants into a contemporary tale of a New World black woman and man locked in destructive embrace. In *Song of Solomon*, the Gullah folktale of flying Africans is used for structural and thematic purposes. Through folk transmission, in this case the transmission of the "song" of Sugarman's flying home, the protagonist discovers the "ancestor" and makes the needed cultural connections between the urban Midwest, the rural South, and the community of transplanted Africans who still remembered that "If you surrendered to the air, you could *ride* it."

Morrison's abiding concern with the African American community was intensified during the late fifties and the sixties, a time when she was "primarily interested in the Civil Rights Movement." As a member of the Howard University theater group, she toured the South and later taught at Howard University, where the writer Claude Brown and the activist Stokley Carmichael were in her classes. A new mother and a nascent writer at that point, Morrison was interested in the new activism but recognized the degree to which the movement "got embezzled by the media." Because she could also remember "when soul food was called supper,"[22] her response to the militant sloganeering of "community" was a significant factor in her developing aesthetic. As she explains, " . . . the community, the black community . . . came to mean something much different in the sixties and the seventies, as though we had to forge one—but it had seemed to me that it was always there, only we called it the 'neighborhood.' "[23]

After she edited *The Black Book* (1974), a project meant to cross the ideological divide between the nonviolent civil rights struggle and the militant nationalism of black power, Morrison's work came to reflect another perspective on the interrelationship of black history and family history, collective identity, and individual subjectivity. What shaped both individual and collective identity was history and memory, the recollection of a shared past, along with "the life-giving, very, very strong sustenance that people got from the neighborhood." Thus, the neighborhood, the community, is forcefully represented in her work. And in those representations, the form-giving and intellectual energy of Morrison's aesthetic is channeled not so much into "forging new myths" but in rediscovering the old ones.[24]

Faith Ringgold's art during the 1970s and early 1980s, like the art of Betye Saar, Paule Marshall, and Toni Morrison, reflects the artist's attitudinal response to the "crisis of black consciousness" during the 1960s as well as to the feminist movement of the 1970s. Ringgold explains,

> I was taught that art was painting stretched on canvas, so-called fine art. And I did that, and my early period in the 60s had to do with the civil rights movement, then the black movement of the late 60s, and then in the 70s I became a feminist activist, and my work reflected that. But all the while I really like to sew, and by combining sewing with painting and sculpture, I was able to use women's materials. . . . I made masks a lot, not realizing in the beginning that I was making them for performances.[25]

"Women's materials" (beads, raffia, and lace) and "women's techniques" (stitchery, tie-dyeing, and embroidery), along with African-influenced masks, music, dance, and mime, are combined in *The Wake and Resurrection of the Bicentennial Negro* (1976) (Figure 3), Ringgold's commemoration of the two hundredth birthday of the United States and plea for the spiritual rebirth of black America.[26]

An environmental installation with five life-sized soft sculptures, five mask figures, and a number of subsidiary dance masks, *Wake and Resurrection* was conceived after Ringgold's trip to Nigeria and

Figure 3. Faith Ringgold, *The Wake and Resurrection of the Bicentennial Negro,* 1976. Life-sized soft sculpture and mimed performance. Copyright 1976 Faith Ringgold.

traverses the boundaries between African festival and Euramerican performance art. Patterned on what Jean Borgatti describes as African "art events,"[27] in which masks and sculptures are worn, carried, or merely in place, with people collectively creating life-sustaining festivals according to communal needs, Ringgold's performance piece has no words and uses mime, dance, and music to tell the story of Buba and Bena, a young urban black couple, and their families. Buba, who died of a drug overdose, and his wife, Bena, who died of grief, are the two soft-sculpture figures for whom the wake is performed. Through the vigilant love of their family, especially the mothers, Nana and Moma, the dead figures are resurrected to a reformed life. Buba and Bena's resurrection, according to Terrie Rouse, "is drawn from the example of African cosmological relationships which held ancestral deities in a state of limbo until they are released through dance to return to the community in search of new lives." Thus, the African belief in the continued life of spirits after death and the black American folk and religious ritual of the wake are superimposed on the realities of contemporary urban life to create, according to Thalia Gouma-Peterson, a "modern folk tale."[28]

In the 1983 story quilt, *Who's Afraid of Aunt Jemima?* (Figure 4), Ringgold synthesizes the expressive folk form of the tale or family legend with the material form of the household quilt to (re)present the folk type of Aunt Jemima. With narrative text printed in dialect and visually integrated into the overall design of frontally portrayed figures, Ringgold tells the tragicomic story of Jemima Blakey, a successful Harlem caterer who becomes a New Orleans restauranteur. The story also includes Jemima's grandparents, "who bought their way out of slavery in New Orleans"; her own parents; and her children, who succumb to contemporary urban American values. "Hardworking and God-fearing till the day she died," Jemima survives in a less-than-perfect world to sustain "the generations in a land." Patterned on the West African dilemma tale, Jemima's story, according to Eleanor Munro, is a contemporary "mini-epic of human pride, courage, and heartbreak," and "an irresistible folk tale."[29]

IMAGE, ART, AND THE SENSE OF THE SIXTIES

In their articulations of artistic intent and influence, Faith Ringgold, Betye Saar, Toni Morrison, and Paule Marshall make it clear that their creative appropriations of material and expressive folkloric forms are specifically related to the sociocultural and political transformations that impacted black America during the sixties.

Figure 4. Faith Ringgold, *Who's Afraid of Aunt Jemima?* 1983. Painted and Pieced Fabric, 96" × 84". Collection of the artist. Copyright 1983 Faith Ringgold.

For the critical and aesthetic theories that emerged from, reflected, and accompanied these transformations, I use the phrase *critical-aesthetic context* in this study. By this I refer generally to an artistic environment and specifically to those ideas promulgated first by the Black Arts Movement and embedded later in the concepts of the Black Aesthetic and black cultural nationalism, which the art by these women echoes, revises, and responds to in formal ways.[30] Although the ensuing discussion supports, to some degree, the dictum that everything in the "last analysis" is political, I nevertheless maintain distinctions between "political" and "sociocultural" and "aesthetic" for clarity of presentation. My intent is to offer useful constructs to delineate the ways in which these four women negotiated the "interstitial space at the crossroads" created during the sixties,[31] how they positioned themselves on the border between the nationalist and integrationist ethos, and ultimately how they appropriated folkloric forms to cross the border between dominant Euramerican cultural codes and black American nationalist aesthetics.

Scholars of African American intellectual and cultural history have generally recognized that the steady stream of migration from the South to urban areas in the Northeast, Midwest, and California, the metaphoric and geographic crossings over the Mason-Dixon line after World War I, constituted a major stimulus for the sweeping changes in black life and culture manifested during the sixties. This shift in locale and perspective widened the gulf and heightened the estrangement between modern black America and its southern-based folk tradition, an estrangement that was felt in virtually every aspect of black life, from social roles and family structure to artistic expression.[32] Equally important, the new urban borderlands created by the migration, crisscrossed with difference and otherness, generated an array of transformations and ideologies that shifted the parameters and problematized the delineation of a collective, cultural identity. The way in which these transformations were manifested, historically and politically, was that after the civil rights or "freedom" movement of the late 1950s black power, black nationalism (including the religio-nationalist Nation of Islam), and Pan-Africanism emerged as the major and sometimes competing political and ideological movements of the African American community during the last half of the sixties.

In contrast to the civil rights movement, with its communal folk frame of mass meetings and nonviolent demonstrations, freedom songs, and spirituals,[33] black nationalism and the various forms of Pan-Africanism sought to establish solidarity with the independence movements in sub-Saharan Africa and the resistance to colonialism by other racially oppressed people in developing countries. Embracing and attempting to replicate the success of the Cuban, Algerian, and North Vietnamese revolutions, nationalist and Pan-Africanist

movements in the United States espoused views of domestic col-
onization and articulated the revolutionary philosophy of Franz
Fanon and the doctrine of Négritude. Thus the ascendancy of cultural and political nationalism, with its emphasis on the urban and
African, enlarged the gulf between black America and its folk roots.

Moreover, as Abiola Irele has discerned, nationalist movements,
in their attempt to mold anew the image of the dominated people,
are usually accompanied by parallel cultural movements to assist
in the task.[34] Within a few years after the first black power chant,
the program of nation-building in black America moved into the
cultural arena, the only battleground, in some estimations, on which
it stood any real chance of winning.[35] One consequence was the
creation of cultural organizations and art movements like Africobra,
the Black Arts Movement, OBAC, Black Arts Theatre, Forum 66,
and AMSAC, all of which, with the philosophical underpinnings
of Négritude, espoused variants of black cultural nationalism and
the Black Aesthetic. Focusing on poetry, fiction, visual art, music,
and other performing arts, these organizations and their leaders ad-
vanced descriptive and prescriptive formulations for art by African
Americans.[36]

In one of the first theoretical formulations, Larry Neal, defining
the Black Arts Movement as the "aesthetic sister" of and the real impulse behind black power, proposed a radical reordering of Western
aesthetics and the creation of a "separate symbolism, mythology,
critique, and iconology." Because, in Neal's political framework,
black people constituted a "nation within the belly of white America," black art should "stand for the collective consciousness and
unconscious of black America" and should reflect the "will toward
self-determination and nationhood."[37]

In a later essay, entitled "Black Cultural Nationalism" (1969),
Ron (Maulana) Karenga argued that for art to be "black art," it
must "expose the enemy, praise the people, and support the revolution." It must be functional, collective, and committed. Lee Ransaw,
in his analysis of Karenga's cultural nationalism and its impact
on visual artists, notes that the relationship of the community to
the art world and the concept of art "shifted toward its visual
artists in the 1960s. Community leaders provided the guidelines
for the content of that art. This was to be an art designed to serve

functionally a psychological Black nation. . . . It was to repudiate the happy-go-lucky themes of the Black experience and concentrate on developing community pride."[38]

Hoyt Fuller, observing that young black artists and intellectuals were "infected with the fever of affirmation . . . rediscovering their heritage and their history, seeing it with new eyes," asserted similarly,

> There is a revolution in black literature in America. It is nationalist in direction. . . . It is deliberately moving outside the sphere of traditional Western forms, limitations, and presumptions. . . . The creators of the new black literature . . . are about the business of destroying those images and myths that have crippled and degraded black people and the institution of new images and myths that will liberate them.[39]

Finally, Addison Gayle, the major spokesman during that era, asserted that black writers were

> prepared to move forward in the most monumental undertaking of the twentieth century—the task of redefining the definitions, creating new myths, symbols, and images, articulating new values, and recording the progression of a great people from social and political awareness to a consciousness of their historical importance as a people and as a nation within a nation.[40]

Within the general framework of subverting Western aesthetic conventions, these new theories offered a set of alternative cultural practices by which black Americans would redefine identity. Thus, art, the vehicle for the reproduction and redefinition of identity, was to record history and cultural heritage. Equally important, art was to repudiate the "happy-go-lucky" themes derived from folk culture and project new myths, values, symbols, and images.

In these new critical and aesthetic theories, the term *image* meant much more than artistic representation. Signifying also impression, perception, and apprehension, the figure of the black American, *image* was fundamentally the definition and presentation of race. For that reason, the new images, myths, and symbols were to be linked to a new conception of racial pride, to a newly "rediscovered" black history and heritage. This was important for a number of reasons.

First, writers, artists, and critics during the sixties, like their Harlem Renaissance predecessors, understood the image to be the workshop of meaning. As part of the human storehouse of knowledge, images in art and elsewhere give form to perceptions at a given moment in time and project future plans and actions; they can shape behavior. Images have a temporal dimension in the sense that they not only form immediate perceptual experience but also guide intentions. Treating the image and creating the image were perceived as useful ways to guide futurity and control meaning.[41]

A second reason for this emphasis on representation derived from the fact that with visual and verbal images, the dictum that "form follows function" ordinarily applies. That is, the intended function of the image shapes and directs, to a large degree, its configuration and substance. The image of Aunt Jemima is exemplary. As the quintessential mammy, the overweight, heavy-busted, strong, and religious black woman who cooks, cleans, and nurtures, Jemima was the representation of the white-identified, black female servant. Good-natured, loyal, and trustworthy, the Jemima image was first popularized at the 1893 Columbia Exposition in Chicago to market self-rising flour. From the success of that endeavor, the image proliferated and served a specific twofold function. The first was to valorize and reinforce the quality of submission. The second was to displace the fearsome, physical aspects of being female—those relating to domesticity and nurturing, especially breast-feeding— onto the black woman.

For African Americans, however, Jemima, like Topsy, Uncle Remus, and Sambo, was a folk type transformed into a derogatory stereotype. Such images were perceived not only as degrading, but as having the function of imposing definitions of inferiority and inducing self-loathing.[42] Thus, a major imperative in the nationalist discourse on image and art during the sixties was the repudiation of the stereotypical and negative images created by cultural outsiders and the re-production of identity from inside.

Because black Americans historically had to struggle in defense of an identity and virtues that not only had their functional values questioned, but also were used to impose feelings of shame,[43] the loss of control over the definitions, images, and symbols pertaining to identity was perceived during the 1960s to have been perhaps the most damaging in the experience of displacement.

Proponents of black cultural nationalism and the Black Aesthetic were aware, then, of the power inherent in controlling the forms of representation, the definitions, images, and symbols that fashioned identity. The goal was to change and correct not only the view held by others, but also the view that African Americans, as marginalized people, held of themselves. The activist and minister Malcolm X understood and expressed this imperative:

> We have to teach our people something about our cultural roots. . . . Once our people are taught about the glorious civilizations that existed on the African continent, they won't be ashamed of who they are. We will reach back and link ourselves to those roots, and this will make the feeling of dignity come into us. . . . The restoration of our cultural roots and history will restore dignity to the black people in this country.[44]

The position paper issued in 1966 by the Atlanta Project members of the Student Nonviolent Coordinating Committee (SNCC) made the relationship between cultural identity and Africa even more explicit:

> The necessity of dealing with the question of identity is of prime importance in our struggle. The systematic destruction of our links to Africa, the cultural cut-off to Blacks in this country from Blacks in Africa are not situations that conscious Black people in the country are willing to accept.[45]

In the monumental task of black nation-building and black cultural reconstruction, the production of identity through the control of representation was a critical assignment. The projection of positive, new, and dignified images was linked to the articulation of the historic importance and the ancestral achievements of black Americans. For both, it would be necessary to cross continental, cultural, and psychosocial borders to reclaim Africa as the source.

The 1960s articulation of "Africa as the source," even with its deep roots in black American political and intellectual history, required a rupturing of borders, particularly those forged to delineate the difference between the "civilized," colonizing West and the "primitive," marginalized other. The several back-to-Africa movements—Alain Locke's "ancestralism," Pan-Africanism, and Négritude—served as forerunners for the rupturing of those borders in the 1960s critical-aesthetic formulations of the Black Aesthetic and black cultural nationalism.

One of the basic tenets of Négritude, the aesthetic philosophy formulated by Leopold Senghor, Aime Cesaire, and Leon Damas in Paris during the 1930s, was that Africans and African-descended people in diaspora "return to the source." Defined by Senghor, its principal theoretician, as "the sum total of values of the Negro-African world," Négritude began as a literary-poetic movement that affirmed blackness, the uniqueness of the African personality, and the *élan* of African civilization.[46] Described by Jean-Paul Sartre in 1948 as "anti-racist racism," the doctrine has been denounced, especially by those writers and scholars in the modernist tradition, as a mystical, romantic rhapsodizing of Africa and as an exotic inversion of African typifications derived from white stereotypes. Perhaps the most succinct denunciation was that of the Nobel Laureate Wole Soyinka, whose response to Négritude was simply that "the tiger does not proclaim its tigritude." Despite the host of radical critiques, Négritude nevertheless traversed geographical and cultural borders to exert significant influence on African American activists, intellectuals, and artists during the 1960s.

The first reason for Négritude's influence was that, in constructing alternative forms of knowledge, the doctrine challenged traditional European exclusionary practices with regard to race, ethnicity, humanism, and art. Then, too, as Cheikh Anta Diop explains, Négritude, focusing on the "primacy of culture," essentially stressed the New World African's past, present, and future potential contribution to the world. Next, although it was not generally well known during the sixties, Négritude, especially with the exhortation that black people return to the source, was linked to the 1920s cultural and intellectual movement in Harlem. Appreciably influenced by the poetry of Claude McKay, Countee Cullen, and Langston Hughes, and also by the apparent success of the "Aframerican" experience of the Harlem Renaissance, Senghor and Damas, as young African students in Paris during the 1930s, were also profoundly influenced by the "ancestralism" of Alain Locke and acknowledged his contribution to the origins of the doctrine. As early as 1925, in the essay "Apropos of Africa," Locke had written, "Eventually all peoples exhibit the homing instinct and turn back physically or mentally, hopefully and helpfully, to the land of their origin."[47]

Négritude's summons to return to the source elicited great response in the nationalist climate of the sixties because it was a newer
version of "back to Africa." And the "back to Africa" posture during
those years, as Harold Cruse discerns, not only provided another out-
let for "the anti-American mood and its modern form of alienation,"
but also, as a "romance of the mind," it was "a balm for the psyche
which had a bolstering effect on black self-esteem."[48] In terms of the
critical-aesthetic context of the sixties, two points need to be made
with regard to Négritude. The first is that as an aesthetic philosophy,
it provided the needed aesthetic complement to prevailing political
ideology. The second is that its revitalization and reception by na-
tionalists of both political and cultural persuasions can be attributed
to the fact that it offered Africa as image and source—of ancestral
achievement, historic importance, and ethnic pride.

In the visual arts, where the influence of African art on nineteenth-
and twentieth-century European art had been documented extensively, "Africa as the source" played a significant role in the aesthetic
choices made by black artists during the sixties and later; as Mary
Schmidt Campbell explains,

> Since the Harlem Renaissance, African art had been identified
> as the natural artistic heritage of New World Africans. That her-
> itage, that ancestral link between Africa and African Americans
> was bolstered during the 1950s and 1960s as the African struggle
> for independence from European colonizers began to resemble
> the African American struggle for freedom in the United States.
> Also as nationalistic fervor mounted and the emblems of Black
> pride surfaced, Africa became a conspicuous symbol of ethnic
> pride.
>   For Black artists in particular, African art held out an aesthetic
> option. . . . The formal exigencies of the art permitted a union
> with modernist formal vocabulary with no loss of commitment
> of identity, history, or political relevance.[49]

Thus, the motifs, materials, and symbols used by African American
visual artists during the sixties and later were chosen consciously to
represent the African cultural and aesthetic legacy. The influence of
the African aesthetic legacy on visual artists was felt throughout the
seventies and continued into the early eighties. For the exhibit *Ritual
and Myth: A Survey of African American Art,* held in 1982 at the Studio

Museum in Harlem, Leslie King Hammond explains that the intent of the survey was

> to focus on specific plastic images which illustrate from a spiritual perspective the development of an aesthetic sensibility as projected by traditional African artists and continued by the Black artist in the Americas [and] . . . point to the vital energies of a people creating and recreating that part of their cultural history and legacy which speaks to the fragmented memories of an ancient ancestral tradition.[50]

David Driskell, for the same exhibit, writes that African American art is "often image-oriented" and that black artists as "image makers" have sought "to define the African presence in American art by creating positive images that reflect favorably upon the legends and life style of African Americans."[51] While black Americans in general exerted little or no control of their image as presented by television, radio, or film, as Driskell indicates, black artists did have control over the images they presented in their work. Thus, in compliance with the politics of the period, the writer was enjoined to become the "myth-maker of the people" and the visual artist the "guardian of the image."[52]

These roles, responsibilities, and demands, requiring as they did a certain ideological congruence, if not actual "obsequiousness," were more than troubling for many black artists. As the poet Audre Lorde observes in her retrospective analysis of the sixties, the emphasis on image projection and by implication the requirement that art and the artistic image conform to a certain correctness, created, in effect, "a new set of shackles."[53]

A related sentiment is echoed in Toni Morrison's essay, "Rediscovering Black History." Morrison begins this piece with the account of an incident she observed in 1963 when the NAACP convention organizers demanded the removal of two statues of black jockeys from the lobby of the Chicago hotel where they were to convene. The artist's response to this incident was a question. "What on earth did the little statues of black jockeys have to do with the Civil Rights Movement?" The answer, in 1963, I surmise, was "image." Faith Ringgold's account of her experience in Nigeria translates the same concern with controlling and guarding the artistic image. According to Ringgold, the black American representatives at the 1977 Festival of Culture in Lagos were reluctant to display her work because it was too "primitive" and "craftsy" and "not at all what they [wanted] people to think American blacks were into."[54]

Morrison critiques the emphasis on image in the same essay on black history. In her view, the attempts to control the image of black Americans had too much of the "spirit of reacting to white values . . . to what they *thought* rather than what we *knew*." The consequence, in Morrison's opinion, was the "annihilation of Amos 'n' Andy," and the "slaughter of Sambo." Originally performed by two white comedians who impersonated blacks on radio, the *Amos 'n' Andy* duo was popularized further on television during the early 1950s, when black Americans assumed the roles. Because many black Americans saw *Amos 'n' Andy*, like the children's book *Little Black Sambo*, as reinforcing negative stereotypes, the NAACP demanded the removal of the sitcom from television in 1966. Morrison, however, subverting nationalist ideology and the demand for new and different images of black Americans, asserts that Amos and Andy were "characters" for whom she had much affection and that the children's book *Little Black Sambo* portrayed a "child as deeply loved and pampered by his parents as ever lived."[55]

Morrison, like Marshall, Ringgold, and Saar, reclaims the stereotypes derived from folk culture in her works but refutes their derogatory and degrading associations through the act of transformation. Collectively these four artists make use of images like Sambo and Aunt Jemima but situate them in new contexts to reflect an African-connected consciousness. They reclaim the customs and beliefs associated with folk magic but re-present the magical practices of conjure, voodoo, and hoodoo as an alternative empowering spirituality. They transform the essential performance feature of black oratory, the dozens, the oral folktale, the rap, and the sermon and give it aesthetic form.

The conscious return to the African American folk matrix by these four artists during the 1970s and early 1980s was, in great part, a consequence of their response to its "annihilation" by the critical-aesthetic theories that materialized during the sixties. Moreover, since the demand that occasioned its repudiation was at once political and aesthetic, the response itself may be seen as two-dimensional.

On the level of individual aesthetics, the notion of "creative tur-moil," a phenomenon characterizing both the act of creation and the aesthetic response, delineates one dimension of the response by these four women to repudiation of black folklore. According to Carolyn Fowler, who uses the term in her discussion of black aesthetics, if art indeed fosters a belief in humanity, "in life and its dignity," then the creative act "recreates the horror and frustration of injustice and involves our whole being in searching for answers." In Fowler's view, the black artist especially attempts to generate an aesthetic response that is not "drained of emotion and at peace, but troubled with no place to hide." In that effort, she confronts "the ignominious postures of black experience squarely by selecting out the most humiliating images and transposing them into symbols."[56] Transposing images into symbols, or "aesthetic transformation," in this sense means that the artist recasts the derogatory image or stereotype and invests it with new significance by redirecting and expanding the perceptual experience it generates.

But because these negative, stereotypical images still represented painful distortions, retrieving and reclaiming them, even to trans-pose into symbols, was problematic. The theories generated by the Black Aesthetic and black cultural nationalism, reflecting black America's estrangement from the folk tradition and a rejection of its significance, still required the repudiation of the images and values associated with that tradition. In other words, reacting to "what they *thought* rather than what we *knew*" was an aspect of the 1960s black consciousness that generated tension. The use and reclamation of stereotypical images, material, and expressive folk forms by these artists was therefore a socially symbolic act, a creative response and action that had the function of inventing formal solutions to unresolvable social contradictions.[57]

Because the political dimension of the response by these four women meant the affirmation of group goals and aspirations, on one level what we see in their works is similar to what we see in Ishmael Reed's *Mumbo Jumbo*, in Joe Overstreet's *New Jemima*, or Romare Bearden's *Conjure Woman*. Ringgold, Saar, Marshall, and Morrison, like their male counterparts, acquiesced to the demand to produce the images, symbols, and myths that would reflect favorably on the experience of African Americans and link them to their historic and cultural roots. However, the images they produced were constructed and reinvented from the "old" ones and reflected the specificity of the black woman's experience as well as her cultural role.

Betye Saar's *Mojo* series is exemplary. *Mojo,* which refers to magic, witchcraft, or conjure, is a term derived from southern-based blues folklore but has connections to African ritual. Capitalizing on "the very natural union between ritual magic of a southern black folk culture and African rituals," Saar responds to the unresolvable social contradiction with the formal solution of her art.[58] Paule Marshall, in *Praisesong for the Widow,* responds similarly with a solution in the formal structure of plot. Before the protagonist, Avey Johnson, makes the final return to the source, the deserted island in the Caribbean where she discovers that though she has no nation, she has herself and her personal and family history, Marshall orchestrates, through memory, a psychic return to Avey's childhood experience in rural South Carolina as an important aspect of her preparation.

In these and other works by these artists, the interaction with and against the critical and aesthetic theories of the sixties is reflected in a series of border crossings. In the conscious structuring of crossings back to an originary African source, however, these works emphasize that, while Africa culturally and geographically is indeed the final source, African-based southern folklore, despite its stereotypical, derogatory images and its painful reminders of slavery, lynching, and sharecropping, is the experience of African-descended people in the New World and is therefore a necessary link in the cultural continuum. In this sense, the folk matrix constitutes a mediational site where familiar antimonies are resurrected and confronted, where borders are ruptured and reframed to negotiate intragroup identity and intercultural exchange.[59]

2

FOLK MAGIC, WOMEN, AND IDENTITY

In fact, the Negro has not been christianized as extensively as is generally believed. The great masses are still standing before their pagan altars calling old gods by new names.

Zora Neale Hurston

We need magic
now we need the spells, to raise up
return, destroy, and create. What will be

the sacred words?

Amiri Baraka

In the art they produced during the 1970s, Betye Saar, Faith Ringgold, Toni Morrison, and Paule Marshall translated folk consciousness and reified a folk aesthetic through the representation of folk magic. Positioned on the border between Christian and African religious tradition,[1] between technological and pharmacopoeic medical practice, between healing and harming, folk magic ritualizes a biconceptual reality. Traversing the boundaries of space, time, and history to connect and reassemble these fragments of the African cultural heritage, these four women reclaim sacred folk belief as transformative and transgressive power. Representing transatlantic crossings and recrossings, folk magic is the device by which they construct alternative epistemologies and legitimate discredited forms of knowledge. It is also the mechanism by which they acknowledge a

33

multiply located female subjectivity and countermand the negative positioning of black women in nationalist discourse.

Conjure and *hoodoo* are the terms used most frequently in the United States for African American folk practices in magic and folk belief in supernatural and sacred phenomena beyond established religion. With correspondences to *voodoo* or *Vodun* in Haiti, *Shango* in Trinidad, *candomble* and *macumba* in Brazil, *Santeria* in Cuba, and *Cumina* or *obeah* in Jamaica and other parts of the Caribbean, *conjure* and *hoodoo* contain a sacred dimension, a transcendent sphere of awe and untouchability derived from the features of spirit posses-sion, altered states of consciousness, and spirit worship. Manifested practically in the acts of healing, divination, and the casting and "un-crossing" of spells, conjure works through the use of curative herbs, roots, rituals, amulets, fetishes, and oral and transcribed incantation. George McCall points out that commercial practitioners of conjure are particularly skilled in the realms of health, love, interpersonal power, and economic success.[2]

Conjure or folk magic and the magic of storytelling, as Mar-jorie Pryse has shown, inform a good deal of contemporary black women's fiction. My analysis of Betye Saar's and Faith Ringgold's art indicates that the same interrelation of magic and storytelling informs their visual representations as well. From her own account, Faith Ringgold's impulse to tell a story other than through visual images has its origins in her family experience. She recalls that her mother, a designer and dressmaker who often collaborated with her on quilts, was also a "fabulous storyteller," a woman who entertained her children and fascinated her audience of friends and neighbors on hot summer nights in Harlem. For Betye Saar, who remembers being psychic as a young child, the occult (palmistry, phrenology, and astrology) was always an important dimension in her life and made up the subject matter of her early work. During the sixties, Saar moved into what she calls "ethnic occult" and began to use African fetishes, mojos, and gris-gris in her work. About her "mojo boxes" specifically, Saar explains, "They refer to Mo-jo women, to use the African word. They refer to voodoo. And they refer to our passage from Africa to, in my case, New Orleans. They tell the historical tale."[3]

Folk magic and the magic of storytelling are also part of the personal histories of Toni Morrison and Paule Marshall. Marshall explains how the storytelling in her mother's wordshop, particularly the tales of voodoo, Vodun, mojo, and obeah, shaped the world of her art. Toni Morrison recalls also that her family was "intimate with the supernatural," that her grandmother kept a dream book by which she played the numbers; that her parents told "thrillingly terrifying" ghost stories.

The point where the creative power of folk magic synchronizes with the magic of storytelling is a point of resemblance for the four artists. The filmmaker, scholar, and theorist Trinh Minh-Ha discerns the same resemblance when she observes cross-culturally how the mother-healer-priestess's "speech, her storytelling is at once magic, sorcery, and religion." In Saar's and Ringgold's visual art and Morrison's and Marshall's fiction, the adaptation and representation of conjure, an expressive, religio-spiritual dimension of folk culture, affirmed the aesthetic of "spiritualism" from the critical-aesthetic context of black America during the 1960s and established and reinforced an African-connected consciousness. In rich and diverse ways, these women explore in their work the interrelation of folk magic and the formation of black female identity. Ultimately, conjure, situated at the crossroads of history, memory, and religion, functions as the strategy by which these artists "sacralize" the female experience of mothering and healing to illuminate the African American woman's role in human and cultural continuity.[4]

Before I discuss in detail the way in which folk magic enters the works by these women, I want to focus briefly on its origins in African religious thought and on how and why this African spiritual dimension informed the critical-aesthetic tenets of the 1960s. While Newbell Niles Puckett's *The Magic and Folk Beliefs of the Southern Negro* (1926) and Harry Hyatt's five-volume study, *Hoodoo-Conjuration-Witchcraft, and Rootwork* (1970) are recognized as the first studies of this magic, both of these works are problematic. In them conjure and hoodoo are regarded primarily as bizarre superstition and exotic folk custom, considered at one time to be an intrinsic part of a stereotypic "Negro character." In *Mules and Men*, however, Zora Neale Hurston describes folk magic and folk belief as a "suppressed religion" and writes, "Hoodoo or voodoo . . . is burning with a flame in America, with all the intensity of a suppressed religion. It has thousands of secret adherents. It adapts itself like Christianity to its locale, reclaiming some of its borrowed characteristics to itself. Such as fire worship. . . . And the belief in the power of water to sanctify as in baptism. . . ." Hurston, as one of the first scholars to legitimate folk magic as a "suppressed religion," subverted the frames that enclosed the belief system as primitive, heathen superstition.[5]

In an early comparative study of sacred folk belief in West Africa and the United States, Henry Mitchell established two additional frames of reference for folk magic and sacred folk belief, which he describes as a "corrupt residue of an originally great religious tradition of healing and guidance." Explaining first that conjure, hoodoo, and voodoo are connected to the African belief in the world of spirits, forces, or powers, a world considered strange to the Western rational mind but which nevertheless has great influence on human welfare, Mitchell acknowledges that this magic is characterized by the blending of normatively defined oppositions like sacred and profane, natural and supernatural, good and evil. Theophus Smith, in his recent study, *Conjuring Culture*, refers to the same binaries as "offensive" and "defensive" conjure.[6]

To situate an African-connected "spiritualism" as the creative wellspring of black art and to give the notion of the black aesthetic a needed "spiritual reference," the critical-aesthetic formulations during the 1960s linked the magic of conjure and voodoo to religion and art. Representing a collective spiritual reference, as well as the human ability to create either magic or art, the suppressed religion of conjure became a symbol for continuity with Africa not only in religious thought, but in art and culture as well. In his discussion of the new black music, LeRoi Jones, poet, dramatist, and founder of Newark's "Spirit House," posits a relationship between art, spirit worship, and religion: "Indeed to go back to any historical (or emotional) line of ascent in Black music leads us inevitably to religion, i.e. spirit worship. This phenomenon is always at the root in Black art, the worship of the spirit—or at least the summoning of or by such force."[7]

In a similar fashion, Ishmael Reed posits a relationship between art, religion, and hoodoo. While Jones focuses on music, Reed focuses, albeit in a patriarchist context, on magic as the aesthetic root of literature.

Magic/Religion came before "criticism" and words (nommo) were the rappings of not one, but thousands of Spirits. Centuries before the "literary capitals" of London, Paris, and New York, Ife, in Nigeria, was the home of the Necromancers, heavier than Solomon, conjurers of dread and joy. Kidnapped by bandits to North America, they became HooDoo men, maintaining the faith of the old religion.[8]

In responding to the 1960s call to "voodoo time," Saar, Ringgold, Morrison, and Marshall produced works during the 1970s and early 1980s that affirmed this continuity, works that reclaimed and represented the spiritual and transformative power embedded in folk magic and sacred folk belief.

Wizard (1972) (Figure 5) is a work by Betye Saar, the "Mojo Queen" of Ishmael Reed's poem, which embodies this magic, power, and spirit. Saar, who describes her role as artist alternately as "shaman" and "medium," extends her personal sense of magical and shamanistic powers to this work, which is full of religious, mystical, and ritualistic overtones. In explaining that her art "has a lot to do with magic," the artist offers the clarification that "Some magic is ritual, but not all magic is."[9]

The magic of *Wizard* is the visualization of ritual and the summoning of spirit or power. In this work, Saar surrounds the wizard with intense yellow and gold hues that are juxtaposed against the dark, intricately patterned middle ground and starry background. The altar and the all-seeing eye (of God) above the wizard validate his ritual, a ritual that Peter Clothier interprets as a summoning of energy from matter as implied by the fire and flames—motifs suggesting energy and transformation. However, with the word *wizard* inscribed above the frame of his activity, the ritual may be seen as including incantation—the invocation of the "word" used to summon the power of nommo or spirit worship.[10] Equally important, Saar's use of *wizard* as both a design element and linguistic sign is an intentional crossing that blurs the boundary between visual and verbal representation.

The image of the wizard himself, Clothier observes, might have been taken from a cigar box. Using this observation, along with the presence of the household electrical fuse situated beneath the

Figure 5. Betye Saar, *Wizard*, 1972. Mixed-media, 13½" × 11" × 11". Collection of the artist. Photo by Frank Thomas.

wizard, Clothier offers a fascinating interpretation of the work as the representation of ancient, mystical power sources other than recent Western technological concepts of power.[11] In view of the fact that Saar "does nothing singly," that her "mystical" work is also "political" and vice versa, Clothier's interpretation adds another dimension to my own. The cigar-box wizard, embodying traditional and cross-cultural associations with the mystical and magical, in my view, is a visualization of continuity. The dark-faced wizard, with his flowing white hair and beard, represents the ancient African necromancer, the prototype of the African American "hougan," voodoo priest, or conjure man.

In *Wizard*, as in *Hougan-Hougan* (1979), Saar represents the magic, power, and spirit of conjure with a male subject. However, conjure in specific association with women is also an aspect of her work, just as it is in the works by Morrison, Marshall, and Ringgold. The representation of female healers and practitioners of magic illustrates Minh-ha's notion that magical and priestly practices were at one point functions that belonged to women and were taken up by men at a comparatively late time.[12] The representation of female practitioners may also constitute a strategy by which these artists explore multiple aspects of female identity, as well as reverse the negative meanings imposed on the image of conjure. With such representations in their fiction, both Morrison and Marshall counteract the stereotype of the sinister, repugnant female practitioner of magic by reinserting conjure to its original context, representing it as an "ancient property," a special power that in traditional African cultures made women into respected and honored members of their societies.[13]

In the characterization of women like Pilate, Circe, and Marie Thereze in Morrison's fiction, and Merle, Leesy, and Aunt Cuney in Marshall's work, conjure is represented as a spiritual, creative, and transformative power that does not collapse into a form of domination; rather, it becomes critical and emancipatory in that it allows the subject to locate herself in history and to critically and creatively appropriate not just the codes of her own personal and collective history but also those of others.[14] Moreover, in their work, conjure permits the constitution of a self based on difference—the difference between the "I and the Not-I," between corporeality and consciousness, the very difference that energizes and gives rise to the overlapping and biconceptual realities of magic itself. For this reason, the paradigm of "inside and outside" as conjunctive duality, as interactive and interpenetrating oppositions, characterizes the literary and visual representations of conjure in the work by these four women. At the same time, however, the boundaries between inside and outside are continually being crisscrossed, ruptured, and reframed.

Betye Saar's visual representations of conjure, the occult, and women are distinguished by this conjunctive duality, by the interplay between inside and outside. *Gris Gris Box* (1972) (Figure 6) contains a black cloth doll with the beads, amulets, and charms of *gris-gris*, another term for mojo. The doll itself, which may be seen as a visual image of a conjure woman or a fetish, is encased in a box containing other boxes or secret inner compartments. At the bottom of the box, the chameleon skins, used in voodoo and hoodoo ceremonies, are guardian spirits or "sentries," which are recurrent structural devices in Saar's work. The assemblage of boxes within a box invites the viewer to move inward beyond the paraphernalia and usual associations of conjure to its secret inner mysteries. *Gris Gris Box*, like a number of Saar's works, is the expression of the artist's fascination with the interplay between "revealing and concealing."

The passage of vision, inward and outward, distinguishes *Black Girl's Window* (1969) (Figure 7), the work that signals Saar's breakthrough in her search for a form that would allow her to explore the sense of inner and outer realities.[15] The black girl, with hands and face pressed to the window, looks out to the world as the viewer looks to her inner self. The nine little boxes above the girl's head, arranged in rows of three, contain visualizations of that inner self: the crescent moon, stars, and sun, ancient Egyptian and Islamic religious symbolizations, represent spirituality; the dolls, childhood experiences and nurturing; the human brain, intellectual, psychic, and creative energy; the skeleton, death; the wolf howling at the moon, sorcery; and the eagle, national identity.

These boxes visualize the black girl's inner self and that of the artist as well. "The two hands," Saar explains, "represent my own fate . . . even at that time, I knew the work was autobiographical." And the window, she clarifies, "is a way of traveling from one level of consciousness to another, like the physical looking into the spiritual."[16]

Faith Ringgold's *Women's Liberation Talking Mask* (1973) (Figure 8) and *Weeping Woman #2* (1973) (Figure 9), explore and exploit the artistic and political effectiveness of the mask to destabilize the categories of witch and woman, and worry the line between inside and outside

Figure 6. Betye Saar, *Gris Gris Box*, 1972. Mixed-media assemblage, 17" × 8½" × 2²⁄₃". Collection of the artist. Photo by Peter Zokosky.

Figure 7. Betye Saar, *Black Girl's Window*, 1969. Mixed-media, window, 35¾" × 18" × 1½". Collection of the artist. Photo by Grey Crawford.

Figure 8. Faith Ringgold, *Women's Liberation Talking Mask*, 1973. Beadwork, 59" × 29½". Private collection. Copyright 1972 Faith Ringgold.

Figure 9. Faith Ringgold, *Weeping Woman #2*, 1973. Beadwork, 46" × 4" × 6". Moira Roth. Copyright 1972 Faith Ringgold.

especially in relation to identity. The artist assigns to these works, part of her *Witch Mask Series,* the magical power associated with African women. These two "witches," beaded and fringed heads of women and their bodies, have open mouths to voice their inner potential, the potential for self-discovery and fulfillment. Externalizing the internal, these masks actualize the inside-outside paradigm as overlapping realities and shifting identities. *Weeping Woman #2* is the image of restrained emotion unleashed. As the open mouth denotes the need to speak or scream, the eyes and tears denote anger and grief. The work may be, on one level, a visual expression of a statement made by the artist some time ago, that "Women in all nations have the same role, to stay there and weep." In using the mask to visualize women's magic in relation to a weeping woman, the artist countermands the familiar conceptualization for both. As Marjorie Halpin notes, the mask, a symbolic locus transcending cultural particulars, represents transformation, a shift from one identity to another.[17] *Weeping Woman #2* depicts the interaction and interpenetration of the inside-outside polarities. In liberating and externalizing the fearsome face of the self, Ringgold transforms this "witch" into another category of being, a being who voices a grief, a silenced inner potential, and turmoil to the world outside.

The overlapping realities of the inner and outer worlds also characterize the representation of conjure in Marshall's fiction, where memory traverses the boundaries between past and present and reframes them. In *Praisesong for the Widow,* conjure, resurrected through memory, protects and ritualizes optimism. When Avey and Jay Johnson witness the Saturday morning ritual of their Halsey Street neighbors, the drunken, profligate husband and his enraged, accusing wife, the Johnsons' pursuit of material success is threatened. They are fearful that poverty and despair, "the real villain" who had claimed their neighbors, also "stood coolly waiting for them amid the spreading blight of Halsey Street." So they make jokes. "Vaudeville-like jokes which they sprinkled like juju powders around the bed to protect them. Jokes with the power of the Five Finger Grass Avey's great-aunt Cuney used to hang above the door in Tatum to keep trouble away."[18]

Like "juju powders," the jokes protect, ritualizing Jay's and Avey's hope and confidence. Marshall's comparison of the jokes to "Five Finger Grass," however, does more than ritualize optimism. Referenced in *Mules and Men* as an herb used to "uncross" a spell, five-fingered grass is also a recollection from Avey's childhood and represents what Karla Holloway calls "black female memory." Defined by Holloway as the "bedrock of racial memory" that bonds black women together through their special ethnic heritage, this female memory is sustained through the telling and retelling of those things mystical to women. Generations are strengthened by the memories of these things and by the memories of women like Avey's Aunt Cuney who preserved them. As Holloway explains, women like Aunt Cuney were spiritual women who embraced Christianity, but did it cautiously. Retaining links with forces primal, natural, and supernatural, they preserved and used whatever smacked of survival.[19] Preserved in memory and maintained in storytelling, folk magic linked generations and gained for itself the quality of continuity.

The inside-outside paradigm as overlapping realities along with the representation of shifting identities as strategy for image reversal informs the characterization of Vere's "obeah aunt," Leesy, in *The Chosen Place, the Timeless People*. A representation of the conjure woman as diviner and prophetess, Leesy is a woman keenly aware of her inner, spiritual self, which is both separate from and connected to the outside world. When Vere returns to Bournehills, the Caribbean island of his birth and nurturing, Leesy first draws him inside their meager board-and-shingle home. But after the "long scrutinizing look" she deals him and his new clothes, Leesy scarcely seems "to notice him further." Instead, she moves briskly about the room and addresses the "silent members of the household," the ghosts of the family's dead.

> "And don't think I didn't know he was coming," she was saying as she busied herself, addressing the shadows, ignoring Vere. "I had the sign after all. Oh yes."—she gave a little nod that was like a nervous tic—"Two months ago his mother-self who died in baby-bed having him came to me as I was out in the ground weeding. Just so. Standing there in front of me as good as he is now. . . . Yes, bo," she said, speaking to him directly for the first time, "I knew you was coming. I had the sign."[20]

The fact that Leesy relates her divination of the "sign" of Vere's homecoming, not to Vere himself, but to silent shadows of ghosts, dramatizes the inside-outside polarity in her characterization. As important as Vere's homecoming is to Leesy, at the very moment of its realization, this woman, who had been Vere's surrogate mother, places him in abeyance in order to communicate with the spirits of the dead, the Old Parents. And both Leesy and Vere, at that moment, are suspended in a liminal space. Leesy is a woman who acknowledges the inner reality of self, which Marshall imbues with spiritual and devotional tones. The ability to rupture and reframe boundaries between inside and outside enables Leesy to endure the ordeal of Vere's violent death, which she divines before its occurrence.

When she prepares her nephew's body for the funeral, the inside-outside polarity comes into play again. In describing Leesy's enactment of the ritual of sprinkling of rum and water to appease the Old Parents, Marshall writes, "Later, alone with him in the house she sprinkled water and a few drops of rum at the foot of the bed, her bed, upon which he lay. Going outside, she did the same around the exterior of the house" (369).

Just as Marshall's characterization of Leesy is one in which the boundaries between inside and outside are dismantled and reconstructed, Morrison's characterization of Ajax's mother in *Sula* is one in which boundaries are dissolved to challenge and reverse imposed meanings. This characterization is a brief but seminal representation of how the inside-outside paradigm functions to reverse meanings.

> She was an evil conjure woman, blessed with seven adoring children whose joy it was to bring her the plants, hair, underclothing, fingernail parings, white hens, blood, camphor, pictures, kerosene and footstep dust that she needed. . . . She knew about the weather, omens, the living, the dead, dreams and all illnesses and made a modest living with her skills.[21]

This woman, considered "evil" by the community outside, the narrator tells us, is also "blessed" with seven children. Destabilizing the boundaries between good and evil and inside and outside is what enables Morrison to countermand the negative associations with conjure and represent a female practitioner and healer with multiple identities.

Morrison's characterization of Pilate in *Song of Solomon*, the archetypal "conjure woman" as realized in contemporary black women's fiction, is another one that refuses to dichotomize power as good and evil. Pilate is a woman who moves willingly outside herself to nurture and protect community and family with her supernatural powers. At the same time, she roams freely inside herself, with a mind that travels "crooked streets and aimless goat paths, arriving sometimes at profundity, other times at the revelations of a three-year-old."[22]

Dangling a mysterious brass box from her ear, selling wine, and owning no navel, Pilate is isolated and feared. At her approach, "Men frowned, women whispered and shoved their children behind them." At the same time, she is respected. Anyone but a complete stranger knew "not to fool with anything [that] belonged to Pilate, who never bothered anybody, was helpful to everybody, but who was also believed to have the power to step out of her skin, set a bush afire from fifty yards, and turn a man into a ripe rutabaga—all account of the fact that she had no navel" (94).

Traversing the boundaries between the living and the dead, she talks frequently with her deceased father. Since she communicates frequently with the dead, and death holds no terror, she knows of nothing else to fear. With her "alien compassion" for troubled people, her respect for the privacy of others, and her concern for and about human relationships, she has a profound sense of kinship, familial and communal. Because she and her brother, Macon, had been so close as children, Pilate assumes responsibility for the man Macon kills and retrieves what she believes are the dead man's bones, suspending them in a green sack from her ceiling. When her nephew, Milkman, is arrested for stealing the sack, which he believes contains gold, Pilate verifies Milkman's story that the theft had been a prank. Skillfully manipulating her image to the outside world with a shameful "Aunt Jemima act," she fabricates the story of a dead husband, lynched fifteen years earlier in Mississippi, whose bones she keeps to be buried with her. Her story convinces—primarily because to intensify its effect and that of her "image," Pilate magically adjusts her height. Ordinarily as tall as Milkman, in the receiving room at the jail she becomes short, having to look up at the sergeant, whose head barely reaches her nephew's chin. After the release, when she, Macon, Milkman, and Guitar are driving home, she resumes her normal height. The narrator explains, "And again, there was a change. Pilate was tall again. The top of her head, wrapped in a silk rag, almost touched the roof of the car, as did theirs. And her own voice was back" (207).

Crossing the border between mundane reality and what she calls "enchantment," Morrison manipulates, in this passage, the reader's perceptual and sensuous experience in such a way as to demand active participation. To "fill in the gap," the reader must adhere to belief or willingly suspend disbelief in Pilate's magic. Morrison's characterization of Pilate is that of a woman who owns her own life, a woman whose authenticity and power, derived from being on intimate terms with the scary face of herself, allow her the freedom to make choices, to make her own decisions about situating herself inside, outside, or in the borderland between. As the quintessential conjure woman, she is one of the most memorable characters in contemporary African American women's fiction.

"SUSTAINING THE GENERATIONS IN A LAND"

As Ringgold, Morrison, Marshall, and Saar use the magic of conjure to actualize the inner and outer realms of self-identity, they use this magic also to assign a sacred and transcendent quality to their representations of mothering and healing. These representations, linked to the unique historic and cultural experience of the African American woman, offer a different perspective on her image and identity as well as emphasize her vital role in human and cultural continuity, the role of "sustaining the generations in a land."

A television interviewer once asked Betye Saar how she managed to raise three daughters and yet continue to produce art. The artist responded, "What's the difference?" To clarify her answer, Saar then explained how giving birth, nurturing, and seeing her children through the various "rites of passage," was, in her view, a ritual, one that was very similar to her ritual for making art. On other occasions, Saar has explained this ritualistic process. Conception, or "imprint," begins the process, just as "collecting, recycling, and transformation" constitute a gestation period, which leads to the final "release" of the work. For Saar, ritual, whether in art or mothering, activates a consciousness of the past that reinforces a vital sense of continuity.[23]

Faith Ringgold, Toni Morrison, and Paule Marshall, like Betye Saar, are mothers. Collectively, these artists incorporate representations of mothering and healing in their art. More importantly, especially with regard to the perspective offered here, they imbue these representations with a certain awe and reverence that in effect "sacralize" the female experience of birth, nurturing, and healing.

I appropriate the term *sacralize* from Hans Mol's study of religion and identity. Defining *sacralization* as the process by which humans safeguard and reinforce a complex of orderly interpretations of reality, rules, and legitimations, Mol argues that sacralization goes beyond institutionalization in that it imparts a sense of awe and untouchability to the system of meaning or definition of reality on which identity depends. In his lucid analysis of religion and identity, Mol implies that the process of formulating and ordering an interpretation of reality and then safeguarding and protecting that interpretation takes diverse forms but is observable in any culture. Carole Yawney, in her study of the Jamaican ideology of Rastafari, appropriates Mol's conceptual framework and argues convincingly that sacralization may and, in fact, does take place in the most abject human conditions. For the unemployed, underemployed, and unemployable in the slum and squatment of West Kingston, the rasta ideology, which Yawney sees as a blend of politics and religion, provides and then safeguards and reinforces an interpretation of reality from which the "functional identity" of the "Rastafarian" emerges. Yawney's presentation implies further that for oppressed people living under conditions in which human identity itself is questioned, sacralization takes on collective and urgent overtones, attaching itself to the particular spheres of influence—sociocultural, political or economic—from which the mechanisms of dehumanization emanate.[24]

The sociocultural, political, and economic oppression of the African-descended woman in slavery, during Reconstruction, and later has been documented fairly well. For our purpose here, we can summarize briefly that the economic imperative of slavery, which required that the black woman function as breeder but which denied her the privilege of raising her children, and which situated her in the constant danger of rape, not only constituted a singular injustice, but also formed the basis of the distorted image and subhuman identity used to justify the transgression. In the project of transforming that image and reconstructing not only a human and cultural, but specifically female, identity, contemporary black women artists have selected as subject matter the very experiences used to deny the humanity and distort the image of the African American woman. In diverse and individuated ways, Betye Saar, Toni Morrison, Faith Ringgold, and Paule Marshall sacralize the black woman's experience of birth, nurturing, and healing by imbuing them with qualities of awe and reverence, or mysticism and magic.

Imitation of Life (Figure 2) is a work for which the artist's stated intent was to "explode the myth" of the African American cultural experience perpetrated by derogatory images. It is one of several violent transformations of the persona of Aunt Jemima during the 1960s. However, with the emphasis on Jemima's womb, *Imitation of Life* may be seen as the liberation of Aunt Jemima from that singular context and as a sacralization of the African American woman's experience of motherhood. The work consists of two contrasting images placed in the lid and cavity of a cheap tin box. The lid of the box contains a doll of Aunt Jemima who stands on a pyramid formation consisting of a "pedestal" made from a cast of human teeth. With a clock situated in her womb, Jemima holds a spoon in one hand and a grenade in the other and stands against a background pasted with an ad for her sale. The sale announcement, advertising Jemima's skills as plain cook, laundress, and dairy maid, also reads, "She has four children, a girl about 13 years of age, another 7, a boy about 5, and an infant 17 months. 2 of the children will be sold with the mother, the others separately."

While the advertisement locates Jemima's value in her skill as domestic servant and procreator, with the clock placed in her womb, the artist emphasizes her role as breeder, assigning the gestation period and Jemima's reproductive capacities a different meaning. With the suggestion that the distorted and dehumanized image of Jemima is destined for explosion, that she and her progeny are a "time bomb," Saar interprets the black woman's role in human continuity as both powerful and threatening.

In contrast to the boxed image with its message of violent potential, the lid of *Imitation of Life* is a pale photo-etching of a sad existence: a black woman and infant in the humblest of circumstances. As the first image evokes a certain fear, the second image evokes a transcendent reverence. Together the images compel a reinterpretation of Jemima's "reality" and demand a reappraisal of the smiling pancake lady's experience as mother.

The healing power of conjure, the protective power of spirit worship, and the sustaining power of female memory are the mechanisms for sacralization in Faith Ringgold's *Slave Rape Story Quilt* (1985). The story in this quilt is told by the heroine, Beata, who is born minutes after her mother, eight months pregnant, is raped aboard the slave ship *Carriolle*. Pronounced dead by the drunken sailor-rapist, the mother mysteriously comes to life when the sailor reaches out to touch the infant. "With her last gust of strength she plunged over the side of the vessel into the deep dark water and took him with her." Beata is nurtured and raised by the healer and conjure woman Lacey, who brings a mysterious illness upon her mistress, Missus Grace, who eventually dies. "No one ever know'd what was ailing her. Or least ways didn't say." As a child Beata hears the story of her mother's rape and death repeatedly and builds a spirit shrine to her memory. "I went there everyday to talk to mama and take her flowers and she'd answer me."

When Beata is about to be killed by Cap'n Carriolle's sons, Winter and Luke, the mother's spirit warns her child and saves her life. Beata is raped eventually by Cap'n Carriolle, despite the warnings from her mother's spirit, and the narrative concludes with the birth of her daughter, Rebecca. While Lacey's conjure and the memory and spirit of her mother ensure Beata's survival, Ringgold's message in this narrative seems to be that enslaved female sexuality is beyond the protection of conjure's healing power or magic. The best that can be hoped for is the spiritual autonomy that sustains the women who bring forth, heal, and nurture the generations in a land.

In Marshall's *Praisesong for the Widow*, the sacralization of healing, which is rendered also as a kind of mothering, is accomplished by the regenerative power of ritual. The figure of the mother-healer performing rites of spiritual and physical renewal, as Carole Boyce Davies has shown, is a representation that informs much of contemporary black women's fiction. Women like Mattie in Gloria Naylor's *The Women of Brewster Place*, Shug in Alice Walker's *The Color Purple*, Minnie Ransom in Toni Cade Bambara's *The Salteaters*, and Rosalie Parvay in Marshall's *Praisesong* are surrogate rather than biological mothers who minister to and regenerate the troubled female protagonist at a crucial point in her life. Experiencing an extreme degree of dislocation that is the end result of some combination of sex, race, or class oppression, the protagonist requires a certain kind of nurturance. At this juncture, the mother-healer provides the nurturance and healing needed for regeneration.[25]

For Marshall's Avey Johnson, a woman at a crucial stage in her journey to the self, rendered also as a journey through collective and personal history to the "source," the ceremony of bathing and anointing performed by Rosalie Parvay is a sacred ritual of healing. In the preceding section, "Lavé Tête," Avey has physically purged her body and has begun the process of spiritual cleansing—the purging of the "stone of false values" associated with her materialistic, upper-middle-class existence. This purging and cleansing, Marshall implies, is necessary before healing can take place. When Avey enters Rosalie's house, she notices first the "sacred" elements: a lighted candle in its holder and next to it a plate with an ear of roasted corn, which Avey likens to the plates of food placed beside the coffins at funerals in Tatum, South Carolina. She notices also the ritualistic preparations for the Nation Dance to be celebrated later on and the sprinkling of water and rum to please the Old Parents.

As Marshall prefaces the renewal ceremony with these sacred elements, she also connects the healing ritual with images of birth. During the night, in her altered state of consciousness, Avey confuses Rosalie Parvay with other women-healers and nurturers in her life.

> The figure had been any number of different people over the course of the night: her mother holding in her hands a bottle of medicine and a spoon, the nurse in the hospital . . . leaning over her spent body to announce that it was healthy and a girl . . . the figure had even grown to twice its height at one point to become her great-aunt beckoning her in her dream. (217)

As Avey's Aunt Cuney is a crucial link in her journey through collective history, she is also a link in the generations of women-healers. In the ceremony of bathing, kneading, and anointing Avey's flesh, a silent ritual broken only by Rosalie's incantation, an utterance that "sounded like a plainsong or a chant," Marshall incorporates images of nurturance. "And when she turned the limbs . . . she not only oiled and kneaded them thoroughly, but afterwards proceeded to stretch them. . . . It was the way Avey used to stretch the limbs of her children after giving them their baths when they were infants. To see to it that their bones grew straight" (222).

Finally, Marshall depicts the ritual of healing and mothering as communal responsibility. While Avey has slept, the elderly woman who had helped her with the purging on the schooner drops by and leaves a "flawless avocado" for her meal. Another woman leaves a gift, also: a packet of herbs to be made into tea that would restore Avey's strength. The critic Barbara Christian has noted that in Marshall's fiction, rituals are recurrent motifs and structural devices by which the writer explores the theme of cultural continuity for people of African descent.[26] While the rituals in *Praisesong* advance this thematic vision, they also sacralize the role of mother-healer in that continuity.

In Toni Morrison's fiction, generational or human continuity, the survival of the clan, and cultural continuity, the preservation of "village values," are responsibilities that the writer assigns to women. Blending classical western and African traditions, Morrison imbues these women, the "ancestors," with larger-than-life qualities to ensure this continuity—the survival of the self and the survival of the community. Characterized with mythic attributes and idiosyncrasies, the mother-healer, the ancestor, in Morrison's works has been seen by some scholars as a contemporary embodiment of goddess and earth mother, as incarnation of the mythic, the divine, and the sacred.[27] Marie Thereze in *Tar Baby*, a surrogate mother and wet nurse with "magical breasts," Eva Peace in *Sula*, a mother who gives and takes life, and Pilate in *Song of Solomon*, the "ancestor" and conjure woman who oversees conception and birth, are such women.

In Pan-Africanist mythic tradition, Pilate enters the world through supernatural means, born after her mother's death, "struggling out of the womb without help from throbbing muscles or the pressure of swift womb water . . . [inching her way] headfirst out of a still, silent, and indifferent cave of flesh, dragging her own cord and her own afterbirth behind her" (28). Directing and owning her life, even before birth, Pilate ensures generational continuity and orchestrates, through conjure, the conception of her brother's son. When she learns that Macon is attempting to abort the baby she has helped her sister-

in-law to conceive, Pilate uses a magic that he is sure to understand—
a conjured fetish.

> A male doll with a small painted chicken bone stuck between
> its legs and a round red circle painted on its belly. . . . [Macon]
> burned it. It took nine separate burnings before the fire got down
> to the straw and cotton ticking of its insides. But he must have
> remembered the round fire-red stomach, for he left Ruth alone
> after that. (28)

As Pilate uses the magic of conjure in the police station to nullify the
strictures of racism and ageism, in this instance, she uses conjure to
counteract the strictures of sexism—to empower and protect another
woman. Like Betye Saar, Paule Marshall, and Faith Ringgold, Morrison sacralizes female experience. In her work, magic, myth, and the
supernatural powers of conjure are used to order an interpretation
of that experience and to represent, on the most fundamental level,
the African American woman's role in human continuity.

In using conjure, hoodoo, and vodun to sacralize female experience, these artists appropriate the emancipatory energies of folk
magic to translate identity. Negotiating the aesthetic and critical
formulations from the 1960s, they reclaim this magic to provide the
needed spiritual reference for black art. Ultimately, however, these
women not only reclaim an alternative, empowering, and transgressive spirituality, they also establish cultural continuity with Africa.

3

RECLAIMING AND RE-CREATING AFRICA
Folklore and the "Return to the Source"

They have instinctive love and pride of race, and, spiritually compensating for the present lacks of America, ardent respect and love for Africa, the motherland.

Alain Locke

It is Africa your Africa that springs up again
Springs up patiently obstinately
And whose fruits ripen with
The bitter flavor of freedom.

David Diop

From Harlem in the twenties to Paris in the thirties to the Americas in the sixties, "back to Africa," "ancestralism," and "the return to the source" have constituted a cultural and aesthetic paradigm for African-descended people in diaspora. And despite a host of radical critiques—charges of sentimental idealism or banal exoticism—this "homing instinct," as Alain Locke called it, has persisted. As symbolic balm for the psychic wounds inflicted by forced migration and displacement, the motif of longing and return, especially during the decade of the sixties, was a mechanism for critique and creation. A critique and subversion of cultural imperialism, the "return to the source" was also a strategy for the "management of reality" and the definition of identity. Ultimately, the motif of yearning and return, as one theorist suggests, delineated a common ground where African people both on the continent and in diaspora could meet and engage one another.[1]

African American folklore, as a repository for cultural retention and continuities, along with appropriations and inventions, facilitated that return and engagement. Despite the early distortions by writers in the southern plantation tradition, the folk matrix was recognized during the sixties as constituting a viable link in the African American cultural continuum. Within that context, Betye Saar, Faith Ringgold, Toni Morrison, and Paule Marshall produced works during the seventies and early eighties that linked black American folk forms to the African heritage. The expression of this idea is as diverse as these artists, their vision, and their works. But it represents a collective effort to establish an African continuum that marked cultural identity for black Americans.

Betye Saar is an artist who has expressed the belief that "Whatever we got from Africa, we still have here." At the same time, the artist also acknowledges the influence of folk art on her work. "It's the only thing that really excites me."[2] Growing up in Los Angeles during the 1930s when Simon Rodia was constructing the Watts Towers, Saar was impressed by the idea that these towers manifested, that "anything can be used to make art." In a manner in common with Rodia and folk art, Saar uses any available material to give communicable form to her feelings and ideas. In *Sambo's Banjo* (Figures 10 and 11), the recycled banjo case and its contents communicate a number of ideas to "explode the myth" of Sambo and establish links between the African and the black American "folk." Juxtaposing, in the open case, the quintessential symbol of the black plantation South, the sliced watermelon, and the image of the dancing, happy-go-lucky Sambo with a puppet, a skeleton, and a photograph of a little girl witnessing a lynching, this work challenges the viewer to move beyond the mythic construction of Sambo to the historical reality of lynching. Saar gives visual expression to the statement made by the African American journalist and reformer Walter White that lynching was "an almost integral part of our national folkways." The jarring incongruity of this piece reaches another level of meaning, however, in light of the history of this particularly brutal form of ritualized violence. Lynching was not only a racist, terrorist strategy—it was also a form of communal entertainment, achieving

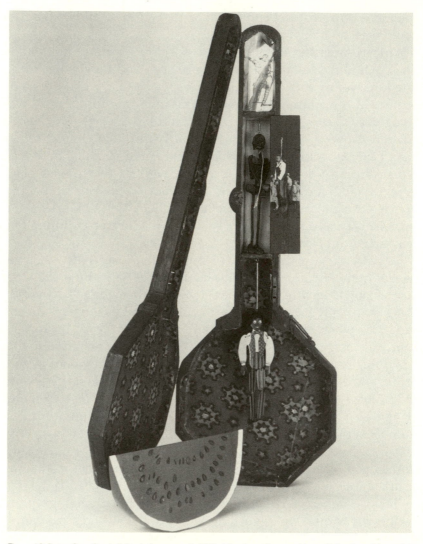

Figure 10. Betye Saar, *Sambo's Banjo* (open case), 1971. Mixed-media assemblage. Collection of the artist.

in certain locales the status of tradition. In that tradition, as Trudier Harris explains, the lynching mob responded "in community spirit by burning, mutilation, gathering trophies, and initiating children."[3]

Revealing, through the open case, the horror of lynching from the inside, Saar joins the ranks of public intellectuals like Ida B. Wells,

Figure 11. Betye Saar, *Sambo's Banjo* (closed case), 1971. Mixed-media assemblage, 41" × 28" × 4¼". Collection of the artist.

Mary Church Terrell, and Mary McLeod Bethune, along with artists like Meta Vaux Warrick Fuller, Lois Mailou Jones, and most recently Sandra Rowe and Pat Ward Williams, all of whom, in the tradition of black women and antilynching crusades, exposed the brutality of lynching through activism and art. It is through the closed banjo case, however, that Saar crosses geopolitical and cultural borders to connect to another tradition and express the idea of the "return to the source."

With its deliberate simplification, stylistic strength, and emotional force, the closed case of *Sambo's Banjo* sustains close affinities to the formal qualities of African art. In much the same way of African sculpture, the work composes voids as much as solid forms. In African sculpture, the interval between forms is as important as the solid forms themselves. Robert Goldwater explains that the artist in Africa works with both positive and negative shapes; carving spaces as well as masses, the African artist invests both with life and character. The vitality of this art, in Goldwater's opinion, arises from the interplay of voids and forms, from their "interlocking rhythm."[4] In emphasizing the expressive quality of pure form in this work, Saar seems to consciously appropriate this African aesthetic principle.

With its emphasis on facial expression, *Sambo's Banjo* assimilates another characteristic of African art. Saar uses this feature, however, for her own political purposes and reifies an aesthetic of ironic signification. In stark contrast to the bold, forthright, and poignant qualities of facial expression characterizing African art, Saar presents the bright-eyed, gold-toothed, grinning face of the Sambo stereotype. The message is complicated. The Sambo stereotype, like that of Aunt Jemima, was a uniquely American creation used for advertising commodities ranging from toothpaste to pancakes. The image, as several scholars have shown, is a relic of the early minstrel show. Considered by some to be the first form of popular entertainment in the United States, minstrelsy was a multilayered parody of black culture by white men in blackface. Through music, dramatic sketches, dances, and jokes, minstrel shows presented a distorted, comic version of black plantation life. As described by Ralph Ellison, however, minstrelsy, "—with its Negro-derived choreography, its ringing banjos and rattling of bones, its voices cackling jokes in pseudo-Negro dialect, with its nonsense songs, its bright costumes and sweating performers—constituted a ritual of exorcism." Offering comic and psychic release for white audiences, minstrelsy and its stereotypes were created, in great part, to externalize guilt and fear. Sambo was one of several derogatory images around which motives of race, status, economics, and guilt were clustered.[5]

Dismantling the borders erected to contain these motives, Betye Saar turns the weapons of white stereotype to her own purpose. She claims this image but situates it in the context of simplified, stylized African art forms. Reifying an aesthetic of ironic signification, the artist establishes her own link to the African aesthetic legacy as a "return to the source." Equally important, in claiming the stereotype, Saar situates a derogatory image derived from folk culture as suitable material for art and thereby legitimates it. But the ideas and meanings expressed in this work go further.

Part of the meaning inheres in the origins and history of the banjo itself, the one original American instrument. Similar in construction and function to the molos found among the Hausa and Yoruba in Nigeria, the banjo, according to several scholars, has its origins in Africa. Both the molo and the banjo, Judith Chase contends, derived from the chordophone, a type of stringed instrument common throughout the African continent. Often prohibited from using drums during slavery, plantation slaves created the banjo, a modified version of the chordophone, to supply rhythm for songs and dances.[6] The "recycled" banjo case here reflects cultural retention, adaptation, and invention. As with the conscious assimilation of African aesthetic principles, it is an element that enables the artist to express the idea of the "return to the source." In much the same way as she does in *Is Jim Crow Really Dead?*, *I've Got Rhythm*, and *Black Crows in the White Section Only*, Saar effects that return by using found and discarded memorabilia from African American folk heritage.

While the closed case of *Sambo's Banjo* communicates ideas and meanings, it is also conveys a single emotional effect, derived in part from the strong visual imprint of the stereotype. And it is the perceptual experience generated by the stereotype that explodes the myth and ruptures the borders framing the distortion. This Sambo returns the gaze. From this subjective platform, the artist mounts her critique of the distortion and offers a new interpretation of African

American history and culture, one that affirms the certain continuity that marks identity.

Like Betye Saar, Faith Ringgold draws from both her American and her African heritage for her creative expressions. As she explains, "I have the advantage of using the American experience such as it is, from Europe, which I was trained in. And I have the advantage of my own cultural classical form, which is African. . . ."[7]

The expression of *Africanité* and the idea of the "return to the source" in Ringgold's work range from the conscious adaptation of African design patterns and the description of African textile techniques to the use of African mystical and cosmological beliefs. *The Wake and Resurrection of the Bicentennial Negro* (Figure 3) is a performance piece that draws on these mystical and cosmological beliefs. With masks and taped music as background, performers mime and dance the event of a black American wake that culminates in a uniquely African resurrection.

During the performance, two "dead" figures, Buba and Bena, are laid out on a cooling pad in preparation for burial, surrounded by the figures of their mourning mothers, Moma and Nana. Through the mystical powers associated with African women-diviners, these mothers resurrect their children: one who has died of a drug overdose and the other who has succumbed to grief. While this work draws on the belief, common throughout Africa, in the life of spirits after death, *Wake and Resurrection* relates in a specific way to the mystical powers and abilities attributed to women-diviners.

As Dominique Zahan reports, these women have the ability to negotiate the boundaries between life and death and mediate between the spirit world and the world of the living.[8] From their own experience of symbolic death and resurrection, they are believed to have the power to transmit to humans the wishes of the spirits to effect a resurrection. Ringgold confers this ability to Moma and Nana. In having these mothers resurrect their dead children, the artist voices these beliefs. Blurring the distinctions between African and American, Ringgold incorporates African cosmological beliefs into this work but situates the event in an urban folk context.

Buba and Bena's mimed story has close affinities to the family "memorate," a narrative form that is common in black folk culture. As the family memorate develops frequently into legend, this work progresses from the depiction of a "family affair," the wake, to the representation of twentieth-century black urban realities. Moreover, with Buba's resurrection to a reformed, drug-free life and Bena's transformation to a liberated woman, the mimed narrative incorporates the degree of human triumph and inspiration characterizing legend. In commenting on her intent for this work, created in part for the bicentennial celebrations in the United States, Ringgold explains, "I was trying to point up what happened to us in the 200 years of our country, and the resurrection was meant to say, let it not happen again; let us not have the same story to tell in another 200 years."[9] In the context of the artist's stated intent, *Wake and Resurrection* may be regarded as a bicentennial legend, one that speaks to black America's urgent need for spiritual resurrection.

The story quilt *Who's Afraid of Aunt Jemima?* (Figure 4) is a work informed primarily by elements from black folk culture, but these elements are linked to an "African-connected consciousness" as well. Using anecdote and black dialect, the narrative text in this quilt transforms the persona of Aunt Jemima to challenge what Ringgold calls the "oppression of the Jemima stereotype." Like Saar in *Sambo's Banjo*, Ringgold actualizes an aesthetic of ironic signification. Jemima, like Sambo, was an image created to objectify fear and guilt, but one that mimicked and parodied the experience of black women, the experience of the communal mother and the female ancestor in particular. Ringgold, in turn, parodies and mimics the stereotype. Her intent for this work, as she explains, was to "make a mockery of the anger people have about Aunt Jemima." Raising critical questions about the origins of the folk type and its stereotype, Ringgold asks, "Who was Aunt Jemima anyway—aside from her image on the pancake box? What did she do to attract so much hate? . . . Wasn't she the one who took care of the children, her own and everybody else's, and made something of her life too? . . . Is she a villain, or is she the ultimate female survivor? . . . Should we hate her for that?"[10]

To expose and confront the hatred, fear, and guilt associated with this quintessential mammy image, Ringgold constructs a narrative in which Jemima is depicted as a successful Harlem caterer and New Orleans restaurateur. Enduring triumph and failure, Ringgold's new Jemima is rendered as the "ultimate female survivor" in all her human complexity.

In concluding this tragicomic story with the question, "Now Who's Afraid of Aunt Jemima?" the artist adapts the structure of the African and West Indian dilemma tale. Like the dilemma tale, Ringgold's narrative questions our preconceptions. Like the dilemma tale, it also avoids absolutes, indeed hinges on complexity, and leaves the audience with a question to ponder. Adapting the structure of the dilemma tale for this work, Ringgold crosses two folk forms and reframes the boundaries for the tale and the quilt.[11] At the same time, she invests the work with a degree of "African-connected consciousness." After Jemima and her husband die in an automobile accident, their son arranges an African funeral. "Lil Rufus brought they bodies back to Harlem give em an African funeral—Praise God! Dressed Jemima in an African gown and braided her hair with cowrie shells. Put Big Rufus in a gold dashiki." Adding yet another dimension to Jemima's life and death and making a political statement as well, Ringgold continues the narrative: "They looked nice though, peaceful, like they was home."

The Bitter Nest (1985), Ringgold's first storytelling and performance quilt, expresses the idea of the "return to the source" through the reference to an actual journey to Africa and through the description of African textile technique and craft in its narrative text.[12] In content and form—that is, through the story, the performance, and the quilt—this work represents a number of crossings: across class lines, art forms, and cultural and geographic boundaries.

Set in Harlem during the Harlem Renaissance and the era of Marcus Garvey's Back to Africa movement, the tale chronicles the life of a black woman doctor, Celia, in conflict with her mother, Cee Cee. The conflict centers in large part on the shame the daughter feels for her mother's unique creative expressions. The colorful quilted bags, coverlets, and wall hangings the mother makes and uses as background for her equally unique performances are judged "tacky" and "mammy-made" by the daughter.

After the mother's Garveyite parents move to Ghana and send her hand-dyed fabrics from Africa, she is inspired further and sews endlessly. Ringgold makes conscious reference to West African techniques for textile craft and art in explaining the mother's methods.[13] "First she selected colors and patterns of the brightly-dyed fabrics and cut them into squares. And then she sewed the squares together in random order to form long strips. And then she sewed the strips together to form large lengths of fabric out of which she made the bags, covers, drapes, costumes, etc."

This explicit reference to African techniques is set against the background of the Harlem Renaissance and the first Back to Africa movement. During that time, when African American material folk forms and crafts were perceived as humble products of a "peasant class," as uncomfortable reminders of slavery rather than art, the mother's "mammy-made" bags and coverlets generated tension among her company of friends and associates, Harlem Renaissance intellectuals. As Ringgold explains in the text, "The times pressed the artists of the Harlem Renaissance into a regiment of social and political propaganda for the elevation of Race people. But what was Cee Cee doing? Was this art?"

In depicting this conflict, the narrative speaks to the larger tension between Anglo-Western notions of fine art and the notion of African-based folk craft as art. It was a tension that characterized the Harlem Renaissance as well as the sixties. Like Betye Saar and other contemporaries, Ringgold in this tale reconciles the tension by structuring a "return to the source," by situating African technique and aesthetics as the origin and source of the mother's material expressions. In doing so, she establishes a link in the African American cultural continuum. At the same time, she legitimates this craft as art and challenges the borders that separate craft and fine art.

Ringgold's challenge to and transgression of that border was vitally connected to, and, in part, enabled by rural black women who founded the quilting cooperative in Wilcox County, Alabama, in 1966, and who, in fact, were the first border crossers. The women in that cooperative, eventually named the Freedom Quilting Bee, who were themselves inspired by Martin Luther King and the Alabama freedom struggle, made and marketed their boldly designed quilts to the New York art and fashion world during the late sixties. In doing so, they not only inspired other quilting cooperatives but literally moved their quilts from clothes lines in Wilcox County to art galleries in New York and stimulated a new appreciation for quilting as an art form.[14]

Continuing the process of cultural legitimation, Ringgold, in 1983, two years after her mother's death and the same year in which she created *Who's Afraid of Aunt Jemima?* completed *Mother's Quilt* (Figure 12), a work in which the simultaneous expression of the "African"

Figure 12. Faith Ringgold, *Mother's Quilt*, 1983. Painted and pieced fabric, 58" × 43½". Collection of the artist. Copyright 1983 Faith Ringgold.

and the "folk" is realized in form. Without narrative text, this quilt primarily offers a visual experience. The frontally portrayed, stylized faces of the black women with jeweled or sequined eyes are situated against a background of bold, intense color—the variegated reds, oranges, and yellows of the women's dresses and floral borders. Juxtaposing and contrasting the subject and background to such a degree as to form synthesis, the work appropriates an African design principle. More distinctive, however, is the technique of repetition with difference evidenced in the work. Each face is like the others but different. Repetition with difference achieves a sort of syncopated rhythm, which is generally regarded as a distinct feature of both African and African American aesthetic sensibilities.[15]

While *Mother's Quilt* reflects conscious adaptation of African aesthetic principles, it is at the same time deliberately naive in style. The sewn and pieced-together panels, the yarn hair, and the stiff figures situated in flat areas assimilate the style of folk art. With these attributes, the work blurs the boundaries between the African and the African American "folk." Using the quilt format to memorialize her mother, Ringgold affirms a cultural as well as a certain "matrilineal" continuity. The artist learned quilting from her mother, who was taught by her own grandmother. Ringgold explains the genealogy of this craft in her family:

> My mother remembers watching her grandmother, Betsy Bing-
> ham, boil and bleach flour sacks until they were "white as snow"
> to line the quilts she made. . . . Susie Shannon, Betsy's mother,
> had taught her to sew quilts. She was a slave and had made quilts
> for the plantation owners as part of her duties. . . . Undoubtedly
> many of the early American quilts with repetitive geometric
> designs are slave-made and African influenced.[16]

Mother's Quilt, then, expresses continuity in the specific category of women's material folk forms. As these forms and crafts link generations, they likewise establish traditions. From the matrix of both black and women's traditions, Faith Ringgold finds materials for art.

THE JOURNEY AS CROSSING

To advance their thematic definitions of continuity and inscribe the motif of return, Toni Morrison and Paule Marshall both effect literal and metaphorical crossings of spatial, temporal, and cultural borders. In Morrison's *Tar Baby* and Marshall's *Praisesong for the Widow,* the movement of characters across geopolitical and cultural borders, however, is for the purpose of reclamation and subversion. Reclaiming an African and diasporic folk heritage, these crossings subvert not only the distorted meanings imposed on that heritage but also the manifestations of Euramerican cultural dominance. Using the structural device of the journey as voluntary movement across space and time, these two novels reverse and revise the historical journey of forced migration of African people to the New World. Beginning typically in the first cities of Europe and the United States, this journey advances to the Caribbean and concludes symbolically at the African "source."

The literal crossings are mediated, however, with the configuration of the journey within a journey and a symbology of place that situates folk communities in the rural south as crucial stopping points in the preparation for the final return. For Avey Johnson in *Praisesong,* this place is Tatem, South Carolina. For Son Green and Jadine Childs in *Tar Baby,* it is Eloe, Florida. These rural communities in the South represent a return to folk roots, to folk values and traditions with which the protagonist must first reconnect, then accept or deny. Defining the character's development and marking identity, these places are vital links in the expression of the "return to the source" as affirmation of cultural continuity.

In creating a new dialogue with the "Tar Baby" tale and appropriating its meanings to the very contemporary situation of a black woman and a black man, Toni Morrison affirms this continuity on one level of meaning. "Tar Baby" itself is an example of cultural survival. With origins in Africa, where the principle character is the trickster figure, Anansi, the folktale has twenty-five documented variants in the English and French West Indies.[17] Joel Chandler Harris's "The Wonderful Tar Baby Story" is recognized as the first published version in the United States.

In the version Morrison uses, Harris's Brer Fox character becomes a farmer who attempts to outwit and trick Brer Rabbit by placing a doll covered with tar on the side of the road. Thinking the doll is human and wonderful, the rabbit attempts to make her acquaintance. When the doll does not respond to his overtures, the rabbit hits it, first with one hand, then the other, and becomes stuck. With the rabbit trapped, the gloating farmer makes him plead for his life. As the rabbit pleads, he tells the farmer that of all the things he might do to him, the worst would be to throw him in the briar patch. "Skin me . . . snatch out my eyeballs, tear out my ears . . . cut off my legs, but please . . . don't fling me in that briar patch."[18] Because he wants to inflict the worst possible harm on the rabbit, the farmer does just that: He flings him into the briar patch. Minutes later, the farmer hears laughter and finally Brer Rabbit's taunt: "Born and bred in a briar patch—born and bred in a briar patch." Morrison has explained the influence of this tale on the novel. In an early edition of *Tar Baby*, she wrote,

> I did not retell that story and needless to say, I did not improve it. . . . It was a rather complicated story with a funny happy ending. . . . Its innocence and reassurance notwithstanding, it worried me. Why did the extraordinary solution the farmer came up with to trap the rabbit involve tar? Of the two views of the Briar Patch, the farmer's and the rabbit's, which was right?[19]

The fruition of the writer's "worrying" is a complex narrative not easily summarized. Set in the 1970s and principally on the Caribbean "Isle des Chevaliers," *Tar Baby* chronicles human relationships: those of Valerian Street, who is a wealthy candy manufacturer from Philadelphia, with his wife, Margaret; with his son, who never appears in the novel; and with his servants, Sydney and Ondine, typical "Philadelphia Negroes." But essentially the novel is the story of Jadine Childs and Son Green. Jadine, niece to Sydney and Ondine, is a sophisticated art historian, high-fashion model, and part-time actress. Son Green is a fugitive musician on the run for killing his wife. Like the tar baby in the tale, Jadine lures and entraps Son. Realizing that her embrace is destructive, Son eventually releases himself from Jadine's grasp and at the end of the novel runs like Brer Rabbit, "lickety-lickety-lickety split" to the island's tribe of mythic horsemen, making a return to a primal, mythic "source."

Through the legend of the mythic horsemen and the characterization of Son and Jadine, Morrison presents her "two views" of the briar patch, of nature and culture, and of the tar baby archetype. These two views, referenced by one critic as "African values" and "Western chaos," are used to develop the writer's more compelling theme of continuity threatened and salvaged.[20] To develop this theme, Morrison structures the legend of the mythic horsemen as a recurring motif in the novel and presents it in two versions.

In one version, the sinking of a slave ship with French chevaliers aboard leaves one hundred French horsemen riding one hundred horses through the hills of the island. From this version, the island gets its name, "Isle des Chevaliers." And it is this version to which Valerian and the other wealthy Americans on the island subscribe. In Valerian's mind, " . . . one hundred French chevaliers were roaming the hills on horses. Their swords were in the scabbards and their epaulets glittered in the sun. Backs straight, shoulders high—alert but restful in the security of the Napoleonic Code."[21]

The other version, which is more central to the novel's expression of the idea of the "return to the source," is presented in more detail. The writer begins this version in the first chapter of the novel, when the narrator tells us that the slaves aboard the ship were "struck blind" the moment they saw the island. Unable to see how or where to swim after the ship sinks, these slaves floated, trod water, and ended up with the horses that swam ashore with them. Some, only partially blinded, were rescued by the French and returned to indenture. From these, a race of blind people descended. The others hid in the hills and were never caught. According to Gideon, an island native who relates the legend to Son, this tribe of blind horsemen rode "those horses all over the hills. They learned to ride through the rain forest, avoiding all sorts of trees and things. They race each other, and for sport they sleep with the swamp women in Sein de Veilles" (152–53). Later, when Son recollects the legend, he envisions this version: "somewhere in the back of Son's mind one hundred black men on one hundred unshod horses rode blind and naked through the hills and had done so for hundreds of years" (206).

The differences between the two versions are significant. In the first, the French chevaliers, representing the order and efficiency of Western civilization, roam the hills to guard and protect, under the Napoleonic Code, the fruits of their civilization. In the second, the blinded horsemen are a maroon community, a community of Africans never-enslaved.[22] Prizing fraternal bonds and mating with

the swamp women, these blinded horsemen sustain primal, instinctual links with nature. And as the narrator tells us, "they knew all
there was to know about the island and had not even seen it."

This second version is central to Morrison's expression of the
idea of the "return to the source," because in characterizing this
tribe as a maroon community, the writer suggests that they have
had the opportunity to preserve their own values and links with
nature, to sustain a different kind of order. The blind horsemen
and the descendant race of blind people, the narrator tells us, had
their "own ways of understanding that had nothing to do with the
world's views" (151). In structuring this legend as motif, Morrison
not only unifies narrative structure, but also develops one of the two
views expressed in the novel: that of continuity salvaged, of culture
preserved and sustained at a primal, mythic source.

It is through the characterization of Son and Jadine, however,
that the writer gives this theme its most complete and concrete
expression. Jadine, who represents the other "view," that of continuity threatened, is the product of European culture and training.
Educated at the Sorbonne, she prefers the "Ave Maria" to gospel
music and has learned that "Picasso *is* better than an Itumba mask."
Featured on the covers of *Vogue* and *Elle,* she travels the "fast lane"
from Paris to the Caribbean, to New York, to Florida. Her manipulation and mastery of the system have earned her money, prestige, and
leisure. But on one of the happiest days of her life, the foundations
of this American black woman's "benevolent circumstances" are
shaken. An African woman with "skin like tar" and dressed in canary
yellow strolls into a Parisian supermarket, removes three eggs from
a carton, holds them aloft between her earlobe and shoulder and,
before leaving, "shoots an arrow of saliva" at Jadine. Mesmerized
like everyone else by woman's presence and wanting this woman to
"like and respect her," Jadine is shaken and derailed by the gesture.

As the insulting gesture "discredits her elements," the image of the
"tar black fingers holding three white eggs" assails Jadine's dreams,
both on Isle des Chevaliers and later in Eloe, Florida. Both the gesture
and the lingering image are central to the novel's presentation of
the other "view," that of continuity threatened. The African woman,
the "tar lady," who had something in her eyes "so powerful it
had burnt away the eyelashes," is a consummate representation of

the sum total of African values, values that are intricately linked, by the three white eggs, to fecundity and procreation, racial and human continuity. As Jadine's color represents a threat to racial continuity, her values threaten human continuity. She sees babies as killers and hates both. " 'I hate killers,' she said. 'All killers. Babies. They don't understand anything but they want everybody to understand them. Lotta nerve, don't you think?' " (175). This aspect of Morrison's characterization of Jadine imitates and parallels her characterization of Margaret, a woman so overwhelmed by the role and responsibilities of mothering and so distanced from the notion of human continuity that she abuses her infant son. The intent is to show how far Jadine is removed from African values and the degree to which she threatens the continuity of the "ancient properties."

Son Green, as the name implies, is a "son" of earth-mother; he sustains links with the ancient properties and with nature as well. Morrison characterizes him as a man who flows instinctually with the natural environment. When he attempts, in the first chapter, to swim ashore, he is caught twice by a current. Though he initially fights against this current, likened by the narrator to the "hand of an insistent woman," he soon decides to let it "carry him." Because he flows with the current and acquiesces to the "water-lady," Son does not reach shore as he intends. He is propelled instead to a small boat, the *Seabird II*, which carries Margaret and Jadine. Morrison's characterization of Son as the instinctual human in close connection with the sea, trees, and currents may be said to embody what Wilfred Cartey calls the "essential ontology of Africa." According to Cartey, this ontology, in which the world of the spirit and nature is "alive and gives life to the living," connects the generations: "The essential ontology of Africa linking and curving through the ancestor and offspring, man and nature, beast and trees, sea and fires. . . . An essential continuity is preserved between earth-mother and child, earth-mother whose breast provides sustenance to son, son who is son of all Africa."[23] Simultaneously "son" of earth-mother and "son" of Africa, Son Green is the character who represents Morrison's view in the novel's dramatization of the tension between African values and Western culture.

He forages the island for food for nearly two weeks undetected by everyone but Marie Thereze of the "magical breasts." And Marie

Thereze detects his presence from his smell, "the smell of a fasting, or starving as the case might be, human. It was the smell of human afterbirth that only humans could produce. A smell they reproduced when they were down to nothing for food" (105).

Belonging to the race of blind people and linked like mythic horsemen and Son to nature, Marie Thereze recognizes the distinct quality of a human smell because she understands the place of humans within the natural order, how they are linked yet distinct. Marie Thereze is also the only one who knows that this "son" of Africa sneaks by night into Jadine's room. There, with the sleeping Jadine, Son tries to insert into her dreams the dreams he wants her to have,

> about yellow houses with white doors which women opened and shouted Come on in, you honey you, and the fat black ladies in white dresses minding the pie table in the basement of the church and white wet sheets flapping on lines, and the sound of a six-string guitar plucked after supper while children scooped walnuts up off the ground. (119)

Images from Eloe, Florida, these dreams of a traditional folk community are the essence of Son's reality and values. These values, he intuits, are very different from those of Jadine who, he imagines, dreams of "gold and cloisonne and honey-colored silk" (120).

Although Morrison links Son to the distant past, to the "essential" African ontology, what she makes clear in this passage is that his American past is the most immediate and usable. And the immediate, usable past, the viable link in the African continuum, is the rural south, Eloe, Florida, with "black ladies in white dresses minding the pie table in the basement of the church." These dreams and images, drawn from the close familial and communal relationships Son has experienced in Eloe, are not at all a part of Jadine's experience.

Jadine is from Morgan Street in Baltimore, and from Philadelphia, New York, and Paris. Though raised by Sydney and Ondine, she has been educated in private schools by Valerian and has no real origins in the sense of "place." As Son cruelly reminds her at the end of the novel, "And you? Where have you lived? Anybody ask you where you from, you give them five towns. You're not *from* anywhere. I'm from Eloe" (266). Moreover, unlike Son, who had been sustained and nurtured by the ladies minding the pie table and by Francine and

Rosa, Jadine had been orphaned at twelve and had never experienced communal nurturing.

In Eloe, when she dreams of the night women—the crowd of women that includes Son's mother as well as her own, Ondine, women from Eloe, Marie Thereze, and the African woman with the three white eggs, who all show her their breasts—Jadine is confused and frightened. Her response in this dream, which the narrator tells us she "thought" or "willed" is, "I have breasts, too. . . . But they didn't believe her. They just held their own higher . . . revealing both their breasts except the woman in yellow. She did something more shocking—she stretched out a long arm and showed Jadine her three big eggs" (258–59). Jadine finally determines that these night women, who "spoil her love-making" and take away her sex "like succubi," are out to get her, to "grab the person she had worked hard to become and choke it off with those soft loose tits" (262). She does not understand that in offering her their breasts, these women offer nurturance and even the opportunity to reconnect, to reestablish the bonds of racial and gendered kinship she has denied and lost.[24]

But the rescue attempt does not go well. The certainty of the night women spoil the trip "back home," and Eloe becomes for Jadine "rotten and more boring than ever. A burnt-out place. There was no life there. Maybe a past but definitely no future and finally there was no interest" (259). Representing a past and a folk culture from which Jadine is irrevocably disconnected, to which Son is just as irrevocably linked, Eloe is the place that directs the course of their relationship and their development as individuals. After they return to New York, the differences between this woman, who has denied her "ancient properties," and the "son" of Africa, who embraces his, become irreconcilable.

> Each was pulling the other away from the maw of hell—its very ridge top. Each knew the world as it was meant or ought to be. One had a past, the other a future and each one bore the culture to save the race in his hands. Mama-spoiled black man, will you mature with me? Culture-bearing black woman, whose culture are you bearing? (269)

Son finally likens Jadine to the tar baby in the folktale, to something "made" by the farmer to attract and entrap. And the text intends for us to see her as that, for ultimately the characterization of Jadine is not a sympathetic one.

The tar baby archetype and the adhesive quality of tar itself, however, inform the work on another level. In Jadine's room at Isle des Chevaliers, Son tries not only to press images of Eloe into Jadine's dreams, but he also tries to "breathe into her the smell of tar and its shiny consistency" (120). The African woman has "skin like tar" and Gideon relates that the swamp women from Sein de Veilles had a "pitchlike smell." Morrison's statement of intent for the novel offers a clue. After she discovered there was a tar lady in African mythology, Morrison explains, "I started thinking about tar. At one time, a tar pit was a holy place, at least an important place, because tar was used to build things. It came naturally out of the earth; it held together things like Moses's little boat and the pyramids."[25]

In this novel, the tar motif complements and develops Morrison's two views of the world as briar patch. It is, as Angelita Reyes discerns, a metaphor for both bonding and entrapment.[26] Tar as a metaphor for entrapment is presented in the episode in which Jadine nearly sinks into the tarlike substance near the swamps. Jadine's efforts to extricate herself from the pit are overseen by women in the trees.

> The women looked down from the rafters of the trees and stopped murmuring. They were delighted when they saw her, thinking a runaway child had been restored to them. But upon looking closer, they saw differently . . . they wondered at the girl's desperate struggle down below to be free, to be something other than they were. (183)

Rendered metaphorically, the dilemma of black American women like Jadine Childs, a woman jaded by materialism, a woman who is ultimately no one's "child," as Morrison presents it, is near tragic. To claim relationship to the women in the trees and accept her primal relationship to nature, Jadine must sink into the tar pit and become like these women, the swamp women who smelled like "pitch" and mated with the tribe of blind horsemen. To the swamp women hanging from the trees, Morrison attributes the bonding properties of tar. Mindful of their "value," of their "exceptional femaleness," these women knew "that the first world of the world had been built with their sacred properties; that they alone could hold together the stones of the pyramids and the rushes of Moses's crib; knowing their steady consistency, their pace of glaciers, their permanent embrace . . ." (183).

In attributing the bonding properties of tar to the swamp women, Morrison presents another view of the tar baby archetype and makes it into something other than the doll used to lure and trap the rabbit. With regard to this second view, the writer explains, " 'Tar baby' was a name that white people call[ed] black children, black girls as I recall. . . . For me, the tar baby came to mean the black woman who can hold things together."[27]

Though she is likened to the tar baby in the folktale where the adhesive quality of tar represents entrapment, Jadine fails to become a tar baby in its richest sense: that is, a true daughter of the African tar lady who represents the bonding property of tar, an "ancient property" strong enough to bond together a people's tradition. A complex novel, *Tar Baby* is a seminal example of how the art of folklore crosses into the art of fiction and how one tale from the African American folk matrix informs this writer's aesthetic.

As the values and traditions that ensure continuity and mark identity are denied, threatened, and finally salvaged in *Tar Baby*, in Marshall's *Praisesong for the Widow* they are overlooked, forgotten, and finally reclaimed. In this novel, as Barbara Christian discerns, Marshall balances the tension that inheres in black people's need to survive and develop in America and their even more important need to sustain themselves culturally.[28] This balance is reflected in one of the novel's thematic developments, that of progression from loss and displacement to spiritual regeneration and balance. Like Morrison, Marshall effects literal and metaphorical crossings, using the journey as a structural device and orchestrating a journey within a journey. And like Morrison, this writer mediates the crossings by situating a fictional rural community in the south, Tatem, South Carolina, as part of the "rich nurturing ground" from which her protagonist had sprung and to which she "could always turn for sustenance." But unlike the sudden retreat to myth in *Tar Baby*, the journey to the "source" in this novel is achieved slowly and with difficulty. In each of the novel's four sections, Marshall's protagonist confronts challenges to her values, her physical strength, and her spirit before she is able to complete the return to the African source.

The spiritual return of diasporic black women to the African homeland is a recurring thematic concern in Marshall's fiction, evidenced
in her first novel, *Brown Girl, Brownstones,* and in *The Chosen Place,
The Timeless People.* In commenting on this aspect of her work, and
how, for her, Africa was both a "concrete destination and a spiritual
homeland," Marshall explains,

> You could say that Africa was an essential part of the emotional
> fabric of my world. . . . The West Indian women around me
> when I was a young girl spoke of Garvey's "back to Africa"
> movement in which they were active participants. . . . When
> I began to write my first novel, . . . I experienced a necessity
> to make a spiritual return to my sources. . . . I think that it is
> absolutely necessary for Black people to effect this spiritual
> return. . . . I consider it my task as a writer to initiate readers
> to the challenges this journey entails.[29]

In *Praisesong for the Widow,* to "initiate" readers to the challenges
of this journey, Marshall selects as protagonist a sixty-four-year-old,
upper-middle-class black woman, Avatara Johnson, and situates her
in first-class accommodations on a Caribbean cruise. To emphasize
that Avey's journey is a spiritual one, the writer begins the novel
with her psychic dislocation. Nervous, perspiring, and straining to
pack her six suitcases, "blindly reaching and snatching at whatever
came to hand," Avey has decided to leave her traveling companions
and to desert the cruiser, the *Bianca* [white] *Pride.* She is irrational,
fearful, and anxious. The source of her anxiety is a dream she has had
two days earlier, a dream in which her great-aunt Cuney, the woman
with whom she spent her childhood summers in Tatem, issues her a
"patient summons."

Dreams, memories, and hallucinations assail Avey throughout the
novel. Jolted by the first dream, she insists on returning to New
York, but after leaving the cruiser where already she had begun
to hallucinate, she is stranded on the island of Grenada. With her
consciousness altered further by another dream in her Grenada hotel
room, she undertakes a midday trek on the beach, which intensifies
her physical and emotional exhaustion. Barely reaching a closed rum
shop, Avey is rescued and given sustenance by the shop proprietor,
Lebert Joseph, who convinces her finally to join him in the annual
excursion to Carriacou.

Suffering through a physical purging en route to Carriacou, the embarrassment of vomiting and excretion, she is in a trancelike state when she reaches the tiny island. There she undergoes a ritual of healing and cleansing performed by Lebert's daughter, Rosalie Parvay. After she is physically and spiritually cleansed, Avey's disjointed states of mind are brought together in spiritual and psychic wholeness when she joins in the Nation Dance, the ritual through which she discovers and reconnects to African traditions and customs, the "source" of her being.

While the technique of juxtaposing dreams, memories, and hallucinations with external reality advances the theme of progression from fragmentation and dislocation to spiritual wholeness, this technique also enables Marshall to link past to present and develop the more compelling theme of continuity and identity for people of African descent in the Americas. The first dream of Avey's Aunt Cuney, which constitutes all of chapter 3 in part 1 of the novel, is the first link to the past. In this extended description of Tatem, Marshall consciously includes the storytelling, folk customs, and beliefs reflecting African survivals to give concrete expression to the theme of cultural continuity. The fictional island, Tatem, on the South Carolina tidewater, is much like the actual Tatemville, Georgia, a coastal community profiled in *Drums and Shadows*. As Marshall describes it, Tatem, South Carolina, much like the actual Tatemville, Georgia, is a community in which memories of slavery, emancipation, and "pure-born" Africans are very much alive. This community, in which the dance ritual, the "ring shout," makes up a part of regular church services, includes a practitioner of curative roots and herbs, "Doctor" Bernitha Grant; an artisan-craftsman known for his carved walking sticks, Mr. Golla Mack; and Avey's own Great Aunt Cuney, whose grandmother had been African. Twice weekly, Aunt Cuney takes her grandniece to Ibo Landing, to recount the story her own grandmother had told her of Ibos who walked on water "like solid ground" back to Africa.[30] Like Morrison's tale of Shalimar's flying home in *Song of Solomon*, Aunt Cuney's tale of Ibos walking on water is a touchstone of black folklore in the New World. With this story, people of African descent emphasized their own power, however mystical, fantastic, or irrational, to determine their own destiny. Though their bodies were enslaved, they could recall Africa as a spiritual homeland, as the source of their being.[31] Marshall's own understanding of the function of this tale is expressed by Aunt Cuney's African grandmother. At the end of her recounting of the story, the African woman always reminded her granddaughter that though "her body . . . might be in Tatem . . . her mind was long gone with the Ibos" (39). In *Praisesong*, as in *Song of Solomon*, the use of a black American folktale that situated a return to Africa affirms identity in specific relation to continuity.[32] First of all, in this novel, the tale is linked to ritual, which itself embodies an essential quality of continuity. More important, it survives through generations. As Aunt Cuney's grandmother tells her this story, she tells it to Avey, who in turn recounts "the whole thing almost word to word" to her brothers and later to her husband, Jay. Passed on from one generation to the next, tales like these mark and preserve cultural identity through continuity and thereby signal the importance of both.

Aunt Cuney, Marshall tells us, understands the vigilance needed to safeguard both identity and continuity. As she insists on giving her grandniece the name of her African grandmother, "Avatara," the old woman safeguards continuity in another, more vital way. As the narrator explains, "Moreover, in instilling the story of the Ibos in the child's mind, the old woman had entrusted her with a mission she couldn't even name yet had felt duty-bound to fulfill" (42).

But in the intervening years of marriage, three children, and a relentless pursuit of material success, Avey forgets the story recounted at Ibo Landing; she likewise rids herself of the notion of a mission. So when she first dreams of Aunt Cuney, she does not understand the old woman's beckoning gestures toward the landing and considers them "ridiculous business." She refuses to take a single step forward. What follows in a silent tug-of-war between the two, with the old woman trying to pull her forward and Avey steadfastly resisting. In the dream, the silent tug culminates in a physical battle in which Avey delivers blows to Aunt Cuney's face, neck, shoulders, and breasts, with her "striking the flesh that had been too awesome for her to even touch as a child" (44).

This dream sequence is as important to the temporal structure of the novel as it is to Marshall's characterization of Avey. With this sequence, Marshall foreshadows a future episode in which Avey wages a similar battle with another Old Parent. The sequence also enables Marshall to characterize Avey as an elderly matron deeply entrenched in materialistic, middle-class values. A great part of Avey's refusal to take the step forward hinges on the fact that she is wearing a "new spring suit," hat, and gloves. To respond to her aunt's beckoning would mean traversing scrub, rocks, and rough grass, which would make "quick work" of her stockings and the open-toed patent leather pumps she's wearing. The great difficulty and challenge of responding to the "call back" for middle-class black Americans like Avey, this scene suggests, inhere in a "shameful stone of false values" (201).

Avey's resistance to being "called back" in the dream as she is being "dragged forward in the direction of the Landing" illuminates also how the text dismantles and reframes temporal borders. Marshall's fusion of past and present, though achieved through dreams and memory, is a conscious adaptation of the concept of time in the African worldview. In that view, time is cyclical but centered on the past. Just as there is a profound and necessary connection between present activity and the past, the future is conceived only with reference to the past. As Dominique Zahan explains, "what is" and "what will be" achieve meaning only as they blend into "what already was."

> Being oriented towards the past, the African finds the justifica-
> tion and meaning of his actions not in the future but in time
> already elapsed. . . . "I do this because my forefathers did it.
> And they did it because our ancestor did it." The profound and
> necessary connection between present activity and the past thus
> appears. The aim is to trace the present from the past and thereby
> justify it.[33]

Thus, while Avey is "dragged forward" to a future, to the fulfilling of the mission entrusted to her by Aunt Cuney, she is dragged in the "direction of the Landing," that is, to the past, to her familial, communal, and ancestral past.

As the journey back is initiated by Avey's family ancestor calling her back to Ibo Landing, the final return is achieved by Lebert Joseph, a communal ancestor, who the narrator describes as one of those "old people who have the essentials to go on forever." The "essentials" Lebert represents, in the scheme of this novel, are the fundamentals of continuity: the vigilant safeguarding of the customs and traditions that mark identity along with a vital concern for human regeneration and healing.[34] Recognizing and understanding Avey's spiritual and psychic dis-ease, Lebert Joseph, from the first drink of coconut water and rum he gives her in his shop, undertakes the responsibility of helping her to "cross over." But as Avey resists her Aunt Cuney's call back, she also resists Lebert's invitation to join the excursion. The resistance to Lebert's call is ineffectual, for like the Ibos, Lebert has "special powers of seeing and knowing." He intuits and meets Avey's objections before "they were even born in her thoughts." And she is weary. "She felt exhausted as if she and the old man had been fighting—actually, physically fighting, knocking over the tables and chairs in the room as they battled with each other" (184).

Marshall fully characterizes Avey, stressing the similarity between Avey's encounters with her elders (just as Avey "fights" Lebert Joseph psychically, in her dream she fights Aunt Cuney physically). Though Avey has learned to control her high-strung behavior, this sixty-four-year-old matron has maintained a certain feistiness. And it is this spiritedness primarily that sustains her through the journey. As Lebert Joseph discerns, Avey was not the "kind to let a little rough water get the better of her" (248). At the same time, in stressing the similarity between her struggles against Lebert and Aunt Cuney, Marshall indicates the degree to which Avey has lost track of another, more essential spirit, how the "shameful stone of false values" has so separated her from her cultural values that she resists and disrespects the "Old Parents." In much the same way Ondine reminds Jadine in *Tar Baby* of the need and obligation "to feel a certain way, a certain careful way about people older than you are" (281), Lebert Joseph reminds and cautions Avey about respect for the Old Parents.

> I tell you, you best remember them. . . . They can turn your life around in a minute, you know. All of a sudden everything start gon' wrong and you don't know the reason. You can't figure it out all you try. Is the Old Parents, oui. They's vex with you over something. Oh, they can be disagreeable, you see them there. Is their age, oui, and a lot of suffering they had to put up with in their day. We has to understand and try our best to please them. (165)

As understanding the Old Parents insures an awareness of continuity, honoring and trying to please them is a safeguarding of

continuity. It is Avey's lack of this understanding and respect for
which she must "beg pardon." Soon after the description of Lebert
Joseph's ritual of kneeling and singing in the communal Beg Pardon,
Marshall structures Avey's private enactment of this ritual. "Over by
the tree Avey Johnson slowly lifted her head. And for an instant as
she raised up it almost seemed to be her great aunt standing there
beside her . . . *Pa'doné mwê*" (237).

While the whole of the novel, in a sense, is preparation for the
Beg Pardon, this ritual, like so many others in the novel, is finally a
simple thing. Like the Sunday morning rituals of gospel music and
poetry and the late afternoon rituals of jazz and dance Avey had
shared earlier with her husband, the *pa'doné mwê* shapes her life and
destiny.

> Moreover (and again she only sensed this in the dimmest way),
> something in those small rites, an ethos they held in common,
> had reached back beyond her life and beyond Jay's to join them
> to the vast unknown lineage that had made their being possible.
> And this link, these connections, heard in the music and the
> praisesongs of Sunday: " . . . *I bathed in the Euphrates when dawns
> were / young . . . ,*" had both protected them and put them in
> possession of a kind of power. (137)

As a triumph of humility rather than humiliation,[35] Avey's Beg
Pardon links and connects her again to that source of power, to that
"vast unknown lineage" that had made her being possible. In the
Nation Dance that follows, though Avey cannot call her "nation," she
can and does call her name, the African name given to her by Aunt
Cuney. With the metaphorical journey to the "source," the spiritual
return to Africa complete, in the last chapter Marshall returns to
the theme of continuity. The narrator tells us that Avey will return to
Tatem and rebuild Aunt Cuney's old house to serve as summer camp
for her own grandchildren and others. And to fulfill the mission, at
least twice weekly, she will take the children to the Landing and
recount the story of the Ibos. " 'It was here that they brought them,'
she would begin—as had been ordained. 'They took them out of the
boats right here where we're standing . . .' "(256).

In having Avey fulfill the "mission" at the end of the novel, the
mission of preserving and passing on the story of Ibo Landing,
Marshall characterizes Avey finally as a bearer of culture. In *Tar Baby*,

Morrison attributes the same role to the night women, the women from Sein de Veilles, and Marie Thereze. Just as the women from Sein de Veilles and the night women offer Jadine the opportunity to reclaim the "ancient properties," it is Marie Thereze who finally guides Son to the "source." Moma and Nana in *The Wake and Resurrection* and the mother, Celia, in *The Bitter Nest*, are also culture bearers. And Betye Saar, resurrecting and actualizing in *Sambo's Banjo* the history of black women and antilynching crusades, sustains the tradition of a "woman's telling of events." In assuming themselves and/or assigning to other women the responsibility of "telling," of safeguarding and passing on the intangibles of culture, Morrison, Marshall, Saar, and Ringgold make manifest a collective sensibility. It is a sensibility that seeks to reclaim and re-create. It is the sensibility of the artist as border crosser, the double-voiced sensibility of those who inhabit the interstitial space between individual expression and collective goals.

4

FOLKLORE AS PERFORMANCE AND COMMUNION

My language has to have holes and spaces so the reader can come into it. . . . Then we [you, the reader, and I, the author] come together to make this book.

Toni Morrison

The call is not the simple reproduction of the cry to the Other; it is a call of complementarity, a *song*: a call of harmony to the harmony of union that enriches by increasing *Being*.

Leopold Senghor

What Leopold Senghor calls the "sense of communion," like the Christian sacrament of Holy Communion, is both ritual and performance. In Holy Communion, ritual, as symbolic structure for and performance of meaning, is what joins believers to each other and to Christ. In enabling temporary release from worldly pressures, ritual also opens up liberating and transformational possibilities.[1] The ritual of communion, then, is fundamentally a performance of alignment and reaffirmation, of liberation and transformation, of complimentarity and oneness. It is a rupturing and reframing of the boundaries between I and Thou, which signifies a harmonizing of the individual self with the greater rhythms of existence.[2] Rites of communion, represented and actualized in the work produced by Toni Morrison, Paule Marshall, Faith Ringgold, and Betye Saar during the 1970s and early 1980s, enable these women to harness ritual for its power and to locate spaces of intervention to create dialogue and empathy. Ultimately, this ritualized "sense communion" is what gives form to their intellectual, intuitive, and form-giving energies as communicative sharing.

Although linked to notable and distinct elements of performance in black folk culture, the sense of communion in the works by these four women actually constitutes an ontological and existential crossing. It is a crossing from the culturally specific to the universal. Following Françoise Lionnet, however, I distinguish recent postcolonial notions of universalism, briefly defined as the "de-exoticizing of the Non-West," from the concept of universality derived from the European Enlightenment. With emphasis on the relational nature of difference and identity and the productive tension between the two as elements shared by both "the West and the rest," *universalism*, as Lionnet theorizes it, names the practice of women who create works of art in the interstitial space between domination and resistance.[3]

During the 1960s, one strategy for resistance to Euramerican cultural imperialism was the affirmation of group or self-identity as cultural difference. Informing the critical and aesthetic theories of that decade as a cultural and aesthetic ideal, the process and principles of African American folk performance reified this difference. The characteristic "response trait" of black performance, the dialogue and reciprocity between audience and performer, was observable in a number of creative expressions by African Americans and viewed as a distinct feature of black culture. Documented in Melville Herskovits's study of African survivals as a "reworking" of African polite behavior, this response trait was manifested commonly in the various forms of black oratory. As Herskovits explains, the convention of running assents by audience or listener to what is being said by speaker or performer was especially pronounced in the black sermon. "In these discourses, it will be recalled, the words of the preacher are constantly interspersed with such expressions as 'Yes Lord,' or 'Oh Jesus,' and those other numerous phrases that have come to be standard in such rituals." Discerning the same trait in black oratory in Dutch Guiana and other parts of the Caribbean, Herskovits was one of the first scholars to call attention to the "African nature" of this convention.[4]

With origins in African cultural patterns, this trait was evident not only in the black American sermon, but was traceable in jazz, gospel music, and poetry as well. In his discussion of the black poetry of the sixties, Stephen Henderson identifies this response technique as one of the structural elements of this verse, which, he argues, has as its poetic references black speech and black music. "Structurally speaking, however, whenever Black poetry is distinctly and effectively *Black*, it derives its form from two basic sources, Black speech and Black music. . . . This includes the techniques and timbres of the sermon and other forms of oratory, the dozens, the rap, signifying, and the oral folktale."[5]

The distinctive technique of the oral folktale, the response trait of the dozens, the rap, and signifying is encountered also in gospel where interaction between congregation and gospel performer is a tradition. As the gospel singer and scholar Pearl Williams-Jones clarifies,

> Audience involvement and participation are vitally important in the total gospel experience. Interjections and responses to singers such as "go 'head," "that's alright," "yes, suh," and "sho'nuf," are common practices which act as an emotional catalyst to spur the singer on. . . . One is as likely to encounter interaction between performer and audience at Harlem's Apollo theatre as in the gospel church.[6]

Traceable in music and poetry, this characteristic response trait of black performance, the affective participatory relationship between audience and performer, informed the notion of the Black Aesthetic. A notable feature in black culture throughout the diaspora, it affirmed cultural continuity with Africa and marked identity for black Americans.

PARTICIPATORY AND PERFORMANCE ART

In their participatory and performance art, Betye Saar and Faith Ringgold consciously attempt to elicit audience participation and viewer response. Faith Ringgold explains that the primary intent for her performance pieces is to make "connection" with the people in the audience, to have them "come and share their joys and pains." She clarifies, "In all my work, I want to make a connection with people to communicate my concerns. . . . I want to in some way touch their lives." Audience participation and spectator response are also concerns of Betye Saar. To elicit and intensify this response, Saar consciously stimulates the five senses in a number of her works. She explains, "For example, I would use some beautiful form for the visual things—something that pleases the eye. And for the feeling or touch, I would combine different textures with each other. And to tease the sense of smell, I would provide a niche for incense. And for sound, I have things that move or make noise." In one of her altar pieces, Saar fills drawers with various sensory objects to elicit response. In other works, she leaves "empty spaces for the viewer to fill in."[7]

Faith Ringgold and Betye Saar make conscious attempts to evoke spectator response and elicit audience participation, but it is important to note that both artists situate their performance and participatory art in a distinct cultural and ideological context.[8] In that context, Saar's participatory-cumulative art events and Ringgold's performance pieces may be interpreted as translations of the affective participatory relationship that characterizes performance in black folk culture.

For Paule Marshall, reader response and participation are important also. Striving to bring to her fiction the "marvelously complex expressive quality and energy" of the language used by the Bajan women in her mother's kitchen, Marshall attempts to replicate the guiding aesthetic of what she calls their "oral art." With regard to the listener, the goal of that art, she explains, was to evoke response, "to make you hear, to make you feel, . . . to make you *see.*" Toni Morrison likewise structures language for participatory reading. Writing, for her, is "not just telling a story; it's about involving the reader. The reader supplies the emotion. The reader even supplies some of the color, some of the sound."[9] Regarding this affective participatory relationship as an essential feature of black aesthetic sensibilities, Morrison is even more explicit.

> There are things that I try to incorporate into my fiction that are directly and deliberately related to what I regard as the major characteristic of Black art, wherever it is. . . . I have to provide the places and spaces so that the reader can participate. Because it is the affective and participatory relationship between artist or the speaker and the audience that is of primary importance, as it is in these other art forms.[10]

The conscious attempt by these four artists to establish such a relationship between themselves and their audiences has an important bearing on my claim that the art they produced during the 1970s and early 1980s represents an adaptation and transformation of this essential feature of performance in black culture. The distinct feature of reciprocity and dialogue between audience and performer had its origins in Africa; maintained and cultivated in black Atlantic folk culture, it was traceable in a number of musical, dramatic, and verbal forms. Viewed as a "major characteristic" of black art, it informed the critical-aesthetic tenets of the 1960s. But of special importance is the fact that audience response and interaction were and remain a crucial emotional catalyst for communal experience, the experience of crossing and recrossing the borders of personal identity to participate collectively and individually in the formation of a group identity.

LeRoi Jones describes one expression of this participatory communality in the antiphonal singing technique, where "A leader sings a theme and a chorus answers him. These answers are usually comments on the leader's theme or comments on the answers themselves in improvised verses. The amount of improvisation depends on how long the chorus wishes to continue." Maulana Karenga identifies the same phenomenon in what he calls a "trippin ensemble." Analyzing the relationship between "leader" and other instruments in the performance of jazz, Karenga first explains how this relationship achieves a certain outcome. "In a Trippin ensemble the 'leader' sets the pace and others come in, or go out, as it pleases them, but in the end they all come to a very dynamic and overwhelmingly harmonious conclusion." Karenga explains that this outcome, exemplifying "unity in diversity and diversity in unity," is an expression of "uniqueness [of each instrument] not [in] isolation from, but in relation to, each other and the collective experience."[11]

This collective experience—the dynamic, harmonious conclusion achieved through the interaction of leader and ensemble in jazz, of preacher and congregation in sermons, singer and audience in gospel, speaker and listener in storytelling—achieves what Leopold Senghor calls the "sweetness of being together and different." More specifically, when the dialogue and reciprocity between leader and

ensemble generates a unitive presence that flows from and participates in the nature and function of the group, it activates "the sense
of communion."[12]

Betye Saar and Faith Ringgold, in responding and reacting to the
critical-aesthetic tenets of the 1960s, translate the affective participatory relationship characterizing folk performance into art that actualizes communion; Toni Morrison and Paule Marshall, responding
in accordance with the exigencies of their medium, also incorporate
rites of communion in their fiction.

As the sense of communion informs Betye Saar's art as cumulative-
participatory events, communion also informs her ritualistic process
for making art in general. In the gathering, selecting stage of this
ritual, Saar selects objects from thrift shops, flea markets, and swap
meets on the basis of her belief that each object is already charged
with the "energy" of its previous life and the "living spirit" of its
former owner. In this early stage of her ritual, an "intuitive eye"
guides her to used or discarded objects that have this "presence."
An interviewer once asked Saar whether she gets energy from the
objects in this stage. Her response was, "Definitely. That's one of
the reasons I take so much time to select which pieces to put into
the work. I am responding to their energies as they move through
me."[13] The response to this energy may be said to constitute the first
stage in a rite of communion in the sense that the artist establishes
an affective relationship between herself as artist-collector and the
"someone" who owned and used the object before.

The unitive presence engendered by this reciprocal relationship
is expanded when the artist arranges these objects from disparate
places and owners into assemblage. As she explains it, assembling
the objects generates a collective presence, and the accumulation of
disparate energies is a kind of "power gathering." This collective
power is transferred in the completed work when the objects and
their cumulative energy, transformed by the artist's action upon
them, are released to the viewer. The spectator's beholding of the
completed work, sharing in the old and new presence of the found
objects, is the event that actualizes the final stage of communion,
for it is at this point that the dialogue, the affective-participatory
relationship, engenders a unitive presence for both the artist and her
audience.

In *Spirit Catcher* (1976–1977) (Figure 13), Saar establishes this dialogue by eliciting a multisensory response from the viewer. The work includes a number of objects that complement the sensual range of sight with touch and sound. The bones and shells are mobile parts consciously situated to produce sound when they collide. To tease the sense of smell, the artist attaches incense packets to the lower level. From its rattan base, which acts as a cage to enclose the spirit, *Spirit Catcher* rises in rough pyramidal fashion. This shape, carrying associations to the Egyptian monuments, enables Saar to relate in an original way to African art.[14] With the ladder leading to the top, the artist invites the mind to climb the work as one climbs a monument. As monument and shrine, the work embraces religious thought and captures the essence of an archetypal living spirit or life force.

Gathering the life energy of the "old, new, ethnic, and organic" materials used in this work, Saar gives form to the idea of communion in two ways. Via the multisensory response, the work creates dialogue and reciprocity between artist and spectator. At the same time, the sense of communion is expressed as primitive exchange, interconnectedness, and communication with the spirit.

Mti (1973) (Figures 14 and 15), marking Saar's progression to the new format of the altar, is a work in which the sense of communion is realized even more conceptually. Altars are structures used for public and private rituals; in both, one must cross thresholds into the sacred space for spiritual illumination or the subjective experience of communion. But altars are also public monuments emphasizing communal beliefs and shared experience.[15] In this work, Saar situates a number of religious symbols on the altar. Votive candles, a trinity of fetishes, mojo charms, a haloed black doll, a pair of guarding sentries, and an array of human stick figures are arranged in hierarchical fashion beneath a solitary, all-seeing eye. In bringing together these disparate religious symbols beneath the solitary eye, the artist suggests that a singular vision, the illuminating essence of ritual, oversees and unifies the one with the many. As altar and symbol, *Mti* crystallizes the concept of communion as a universal experience of spiritual devotion, as the pan-human experience of ritual.

With the transformation of *Mti* into a cumulative-participatory event in 1977 (Figure 15), Saar gives concrete expression to the notion of communion. In a note placed beside the altar, the artist invited the

Figure 13. Betye Saar, *Spirit Catcher*, 1976–1977. Mixed media, 45" × 18" × 18". Collection of the artist.

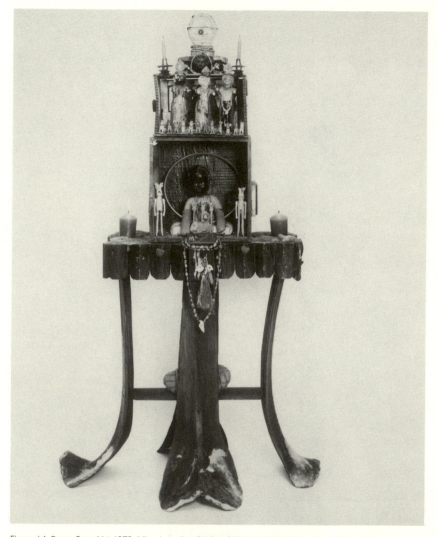

Figure 14. Betye Saar, *Mti*, 1973. Mixed media, 42½" × 23½" × 17½". Collection of the artist.

viewer to leave a "sacrifice," to contribute a gift or "offering" to the altar. Later, she described the response to the invitation. "Within a few weeks, the platform was covered with a variety of objects. Some were especially made, such as art objects, poems. Some 'treasures' from the viewer's past were offered. Photos, toys, cards, buttons,

Figure 15. Betye Saar, *Mti*, 1976–1977. As a cumulative-participatory art event. Collection of the artist.

coins . . . junk from pockets and purses."[16] In eliciting these concrete responses, the artist established a dialogue between herself and her audience, engendered a participatory spirit of unity, and actualized the concept of communion as the process of people collectively creating art.

In responding to the 1960s notion of collective, "community" art, to the call of dialogue and reciprocity, Saar actualizes the sense of communion as a kind of power—the power to elicit active response. As Peter Clothier discerns, it is also the power to catch other spirits and essences and blend them into a common vision and action.[17] Ultimately, it is the power of the artist to communicate, through aesthetic form, with other humans.

Faith Ringgold's *No Name Performance II* (1984) is a multimedia performance piece in which Ringgold herself enhances her attire with an African mask and a beaded ankle bracelet, dances, and chants her own experience as a black woman artist. In describing her manipulation of media and audience, Ringgold explains,

> I have them touch people on all sides. I give them a dance period with some good hard-core dancing music—Lionel Ritchie, Donna Summer, Chaka Khan. I get them out of their seats. I'm moving, making noise, my ankles are rattling, I'm provoking them. I have them making friends all over the audience and by the end of the piece they take over the stage and I leave.[18]

In this work, as in *The Wake and Resurrection of the Bicentennial Negro*, Ringgold consciously adapts West African ritual performance to actualize the notion of celebratory communion. Using costume, music, mime, and dance, these multimedia pieces provoke audience response and participation to engender an affective unitive presence. The notion of communion enters Ringgold's performance art as celebratory human fellowship, as the creation in place and time, of a "we" rather than "I" identity.

In her narrative quilts, the sense of communion is realized differently and reflects the intersection of Ringgold's black and feminist aesthetic sensibilities. The quilt, a material folk form derived from women's culture, is a collective creation that represents the piecing together of material fragments of individual women's skills and handiwork into a whole. In the context of women's culture, the structural format of the quilt expresses the sense of communion as "connectedness"—as a material representation of the relational nexuses that inform women's socialization, women's traditions, and women's experience.

At the same time, Ringgold's story quilts actualize communion in the specific category and context of black culture. Through the medium of quilted fabric construction, the painted grid of black portraits, and the hand-printed narrative text, the sense of communion is realized through dialogue and reciprocity between artist as performer and spectator as audience.

First, the medium of fabric construction, appealing to the tactile sense, evokes an emotional and physical response. The response elicited by fabric construction is what Michael James calls the "touch reflex." In James's view, since fabric and the feel of fabric are an integral part of daily life, quilts, even when hung on gallery walls, do not distance the viewer in the same way as traditional painting or easel art. The physical substance and apparent craft of the quilt not only construct bridges to popular appreciation, but they also foster an awareness of the connection between artistic creation and real experience.[19]

Building on the "touch reflex," Ringgold raises the degree of viewer response in quilts like *Who's Afraid of Aunt Jemima?* (Figure 4), *Street Story Quilt*, and *Echoes of Harlem* by squaring off the array of black portraits in a grid. As Eleanor Munro explains, the grid, matching itself to the perceiving apparatus in the brain that records upright and horizontal forms first, "locks the viewer's mind to the looked-at reality." In these works, the frontally portrayed, colorfully clothed black figures stare out at the viewer. This eye-to-eye contact complements what has been called the "psychic pull" of the black face. The consequence is a visual dialogue between the spectator and the individual portraits that prolongs spectator response. Viewers are permitted to indulge their curiosity about the look of other people and to stand and stare at these portraits to their heart's content.[20]

The narrative text of the quilts evokes spectator response in another way. Because it is hand-printed and frequently in black dialect, the text draws the viewer in close. As a running commentary, Ringgold's narratives generally explain, but sometimes ignore or downright contradict the surrounding visual images. To construct the narrative, the percipient must follow the numbered panels and read the printed text, but is compelled time and time again to stop and interact with the visual images around it. The effect is a powerful dualistic response. In demanding yet another kind of participation, Ringgold's hand-printed text builds on the tactile and visual response to the quilt to intensify viewer participation and establish the dialogue between the spectator and the artist.

In the stories themselves, with characters like Aunt Jemima, Lil Rufus, Ma Tweedy, A. J. (short for Abraham Lincoln Jones), and Big Al living the drama of everyday black life, the sense of communion is realized in Ringgold's depiction of community. Typically, the stories begin with catastrophe. The narrative in *Flag Story Quilt* begins, "Memphis Cooley's Ma and Pa ain never been no fools. They know'd they son ain commit no murder an raping. How he gonna slash some girl's throat an throw her in the Harlem River and he ain' got no arms? How he gonna rape her sittin' in a wheel chair paralyzed from the waist down?" *Street Story Quilt* opens, "Ain nobody on this street gonna ever forget that accident. All them cars piled up right outside this door. An everybody in 'em dead but Big Al." And the opening line of *Slave Rape Story Quilt* is, "Mama was eight months pregnant when he raped her."

Disaster in these narratives is the catalyst that activates the unitive, communal bond that nurtures and protects the victim. This bond, anchoring the individuals in the larger organic identity of the community, is what enables them to resist, defend, and survive. As Gregory Galligan discerns, the quilt is not only a structural format by which Ringgold visually organizes her group portraits, but it is also a metaphor for the communal bonds that hold together these individuals as a common people.[21]

The tales in Ringgold's quilts, depicting the bonding presence that flows from and participates in the nature and function of the community, express the sense of communion in a way that perhaps only the artist as storyteller can. As the artist explains, the impulse to tell stories derives from her desire to replicate the experience of communicative sharing. "I'm inspired by people's quests, powers and life struggles and I like to share my own stories with them."[22]

RITUALS OF UNITIVE PRESENCE AND RELEASE

Viewed as a "performance of the word," Morrison's and Marshall's fiction may be said to actualize communion through language. Both writers consciously strive for reader response and participation through the written word. The notion of communion, however, enters the fiction by these writers at another level. In the organization of narrative structure and the presentation of character, in thematic definitions and inquiry, both writers explore the nature and function of communion as a fundamentally human rite. Communion as the ritualistic expression of human collectivity in unitive presence informs the fiction by these two women in diverse ways. In Marshall's fiction, rites of communion engender a wide "confraternity" or resurrect an age-old "collective heart," both of which have endless capacity for resurgence. In Morrison's fiction, rites of communal bonding and unitive presence anchor the individual in the larger, organic identity of the group and generate the power of human collectivity to effect psychic release and renewal. For both Morrison and Marshall, communion is finally the sign of continuity.

Psychic liberation leading to definition of the individual and group through rites of communion is a recurring thematic strand in *Song of Solomon* and *Sula*. The representation of these rites enables Morrison not only to define the individual in relation to community but to define community as well. Within the specific context of the African American community, these rites of human interaction and connectedness affirm cultural identity as they develop and extend Morrison's perspective on the human condition.

Song of Solomon opens with a bizarre event around which a wholly new collectivity comes into being. When Robert Smith posts the date and time of his proposed flight from the roof of Mercy Hospital, the unitive presence of the "not more than forty or fifty" people gathered is festive. The scene is rich with sensory details. To the visual image of Mr. Smith's blue silk wings and the red velvet rose petals spilled onto the snow, Morrison adds the defining music of Pilate's song. For the group gathered below Mercy Hospital, Morrison renders the scene as a genial, social event. For the hospital people above, the narrator notes that the same scene is perceived as ritual. "The sight of Mr. Smith and his wide blue wings transfixed them for a few seconds, as did the woman's singing and the roses strewn about. Some of them thought briefly that this was probably some form of worship" (6).

The mood of this communal assemblage changes from gay and festive to anxious and nervous as the group recalls its abusive treatment of Mr. Smith. An agent of the North Carolina Mutual Life Insurance Company, a man who was heavily associated with receipts, illness, and death, Robert Smith had served as scapegoat for their individual and collective frustrations. Through this ritual of sharing and interaction, the group finally understands the pathetic isolation of this "probably nice man" who, having "seen the rose petals, heard the music . . . leaped on into the air."

Placing this absurd rite of communion at the very beginning of the novel enables Morrison to characterize and define community in relation to continuity as a specifically temporal phenomenon—to past, present, and future. As Robert Smith's suicide flows from the history and nature of the community (we learn later that he had been one of the Seven Days, a group of activist, avenging black men), it functions also to mark its future. The episode draws together the past (through Pilate's song of Shalimar or Sugarman, the African who flew home) and the future (for Milkman is born the next morning) into the present.

In that time and place, the writer begins the novel, a work that charts the progression of individual and community to a visceral understanding of the past. This understanding of the past, a retrieval of history, is a crucial factor in the novel's development of the themes of identity and continuity. For as the unraveling of history marks identity for individual, family, and community in *Song of Solomon*, it also resurrects the links that establish generational and cultural continuity.

In the same opening chapter of this novel, Morrison structures the episode of the drunken, sex-starved Henry Porter, perched with a shotgun in the attic window of one of Macon's rent houses and demanding a woman. Again, the alienated, isolated individual, the would-be scapegoat and victim, is the catalyst for communion. Porter, like Robert Smith, draws a crowd. Smaller and composed primarily of women from the rooming house, the assemblage here responds collectively to Henry Porter's demand with taunt and jest. Bizarre, yet understandable, Porter's demands effect a call to unity— a unity of the roomers in Macon's house against generalized despair and oppression, against the specific exploitation they suffer from Macon's greed. Before he passes out and falls asleep, Porter voices that unified complaint. "And you . . . you the worst. You need killin, you really *need* killin'. You know why? Well, I'm gonna tell you why. I *know* why. Everybody . . ." (26). This episode, another absurd rite of human interaction and connectedness, generates psychic release for the group. The release for Porter is not only psychic, but also physical. In order to ensure participation, Morrison uses the technique of requiring the reader to suspend disbelief, having Porter urinate over the heads of the assembled group for more than an hour.

Witnessing the release of despair by the group that had come into being around the perched Henry Porter, Macon Dead is forced to confront his inadequacies and begins to redefine himself. "Tired and irritable" when he walks from the scene, he wanders aimlessly until he finds himself outside Pilate's window. There he witnesses a very different kind of gathering, a different kind of communion—three women in his family singing. For Macon, who at that point "wanted no conversation, no witness," but just a "bit of music," Pilate's contralto and Reba's soprano pull him like "a carpet tack under the influence of a magnet." Witnessing this rite of communion through song effects a psychic release for Macon. "Near the window, hidden by the dark, he felt the irritability of the day drain from him and relished the effortless beauty of the women singing in the candlelight" (29). Morrison concludes the chapter with Macon "softened under the weight of memory and music." In using these rituals of human connectedness to present Macon's character, the writer gives him complexity. Through rites of communion in this first chapter, Morrison characterizes Macon as a man driven primarily by greed and power, but finally as a man anchored still in the larger organic identity of family and community.

Assisting in the presentation of character and the definition of community, rites of unitive presence and bonding in *Song of Solomon* and *Sula* are bizarre, absurd rituals because, in these works, Morrison defines both individual and community in relation to a surrounding chaos and disorder. For that reason, scapegoats, victims, and pariahs are essential. In *Sula*, as in *Song of Solomon*, the town pariah/victim functions as catalyst for communal rites that provide psychic release and rehabilitation.

In *Sula*, both Shadrack and Sula are such catalysts. Both are the socially alienated scapegoats who engender a unificatory presence, one based on fear and hatred, but one that nurtures and sustains, in absurd fashion, human collectivity. At the beginning of this novel, as in *Song of Solomon*, Morrison structures a bizarre episode, one that is initiated by a scapegoat and one that involves death. Here the ritual of the absurd is National "Suicide Day," instituted in 1920 by the messianic pariah, Shadrack. Driven insane from witnessing the human carnage of World War I, Shadrack institutes Suicide Day as a day of voluntary human destruction, a day when everyone is given the opportunity to confront death. With the opportunity to confront death and the fear of it (a fear actually of the unknown, the unexpected and the uncontrollable),[23] Shadrack reasons that people would be released of that fear.

As Suicide Day makes a place for death and fear, the inhabitants of the Bottom make a place for Shadrack's annual parade. It becomes "part of the fabric of life." Though for many years, Shadrack is the only celebrant, Suicide Day nurtures and sustains the collectivity of the neighborhood. Shadrack's parade not only forces the inhabitants of the Bottom to recognize the social and psychic alienation of its creator, but also begins for them the process of definition. "They were mightily preoccupied with . . . each other, wondering even as early as 1920 what Shadrack was all about, what that little girl Sula who grew into a woman in their town was all about, and what they themselves were all about" (6).

As the community defines itself in relation to Shad and Sula, human embodiments of the unknown and the uncontrollable, Morrison, in turn, defines community in relation to its hatred and fear of the unknown and uncontrollable. Because Suicide Day offers release from that hatred and fear and engenders a rehabilitating unity, Morrison situates this communal rite as a recurrent episode in *Sula*. It begins and concludes the novel. The death of the child Chicken Little, in contrast, is structured as a central, climactic episode, which, as several critics have noted, is a most difficult and puzzling part of the novel. My reading is that the death of Chicken Little is a rite of communion also, one that illuminates Morrison's conceptualization of communion as the expression and release of the repressed, mysterious forces at work in the collective human psyche and one that enables her to define community in specific relation to the "ancestor."

The essential context for this perspective includes a complex of interrelated components: Morrison's own expressions on the importance and vital role of the ancestor in her fiction; the signal importance of the child in relation to the ancestor; and the relationship between sacrifice, ancestor, "life force," and the concept of communion as it informs African religious thought and spirituality.

First, from her own analysis of contemporary African American fiction, Morrison concludes that the absence or presence of the "ancestor" is "one of those interesting aspects of the continuum in Black or African American art."

> And these ancestors are not just parents, they are sort of timeless people whose relationships to the characters are benevolent, instructive, protective, and they provide a certain kind of wisdom. . . . It was the absence of the ancestor that was threatening, and it caused huge destruction and disarray in the novel. . . . But actually it is if we don't keep in touch with the ancestor that we are, in fact, lost.[24]

Explaining the importance of the child in relations with the ancestor, Wilfred Cartey records that "through the little child life force flows. . . . In African belief, the child is close to the ancestors [and] . . . can communicate with the spirit of her father or with spirit of her father's father." Activating and actualizing the wisdom, power, and life force of the ancestor, Janheinz Jahn explains, are not only the functions of sacrifice, but the essence of communion. "Sacrifice is above all a way to enter into relations with the Ancestor, the dialogue of Thee and Me. . . . This communion extends to identification, in such a way, that by inverse movement, the force of the Ancestor flows into sacrifices and into the community which he embodies." Finally, Dominique Zahan tells us that in addition to establishing relations with the ancestor, sacrifice functions also to provide "moments of rest," "necessary stopping points." In this context, sacrifice activates "an astonishing sense of life which [in their eyes] could only be fully realized if interrupted by momentary stopping points. Instead of diminishing and weakening life, these moments of rest give it new vigor each time, to the extent that life continues reinforced and renewed after each ordeal."[25] Viewed in this context, Sula's accidental drowning of Chicken Little can be interpreted as a rite of sacrificial communion, as a "necessary stopping point" through which the power and wisdom of the ancestor renew and invigorate communal life, through which the weakened and diminished sense of life for Sula, as individual, is given new vigor.

The drowning of Chicken Little occurs in 1922, long after Sula has discovered that because she was "neither white nor male . . . all freedom and triumph was forbidden." But 1922 is also the year Eva burns her drug-addicted son and the year that Sula learns that although her mother "loves" her, she does not "like" her. For Sula, with this diminished, weakened sense of life, the death of Chicken Little establishes a lifelong unitive bond between her and Nel and between her and the only witness to the drowning, Shadrack.

As Chicken Little's death unifies Sula, Nel, and Shadrack in collective guilt and awareness of the uncontrollable, the child's funeral unifies the community in grief. Collectively experiencing the "oldest and most devastating pain there is," they rock and sway in "rivulets of grief." Moreover, " . . . when they thought of all that life and death locked into that little, closed coffin they danced and screamed, not to protest God's will but to acknowledge and confirm once more their conviction that the only way to avoid the Hand of God is to get in it" (66).

After Chicken Little's death, life renewed and invigorated continues for nearly two decades in the Bottom until Sula returns, accompanied by a plague of robins. Embodying all that Shadrack's Suicide Day commemorates, the unknown, the unexpected, and the uncontrollable, Sula's presence unifies the community. "They bond together in collective conviction of her evil which . . . changed them in accountable yet mysterious ways. Once the source of their personal misfortune was identified, they had leave to protect and love one another . . . and in general band together against the devil in their midst" (117–18). Just as Suicide Day 1920, a communal rite of release and rehabilitation, begins the novel, Suicide Day 1941, a ritual of communion and absolution, concludes the work. Here again, Shadrack's presence is catalytic. Twenty years earlier, on the riverbank where Sula's "one major feeling of responsibility had been exorcised," Shadrack had absolved her with the word, "Always." This word, the most important utterance Morrison allows the character of Shadrack, in the interpretive perspective offered here, is a chant of absolution, a message meant to convince and assure the frightened girl, Sula, of continuity in the face of chaos, change, and disorder.

On Suicide Day 1941, when Shad leads the inhabitants of the Bottom to their watery deaths at the mouth of the unfinished tunnel, he absolves them of the fear, hatred, and scapegoating that had functioned to structure chaos. Released from his insanity and transfigured from scapegoat to messiah, Shadrack stands high upon the bank ringing his bell as he watches his prophecy fulfilled.

Although rites of human connectedness in this novel reach into the hidden and mysterious recesses of the collective human psyche, they are nevertheless rites of release and rehabilitation. In the face of disorder and chaos, of the unknown and the uncontrollable, the rites of communion in *Sula* resurrect the ancestor to actualize an astonishing, primordial sense of life and activate the power and capacity of collective humanity for endless resurgence and continuity.

STAYING THE COURSE OF HISTORY

In Paule Marshall's fiction, thematic definitions of human continuity are linked to those of cultural continuity, to the writer's recurrent inquiry into the notion of "collective humanity," and to what people can or must do with the past. Rituals affirming human will and purposefulness are presented time and time again in her novels to define and develop character and to demonstrate that the resurrection of the past is also the resurrection of the "collective heart." This age-old collective heart and an immense human confraternity are what finally enables Marshall's characters to survive and endure, to "stay the course of history."

In *Praisesong for the Widow,* rites of communion recollected from the past and enacted in the present enable the protagonist, Avey Johnson, to discover and connect with the collective heart. Avey's first encounter with this ritualized human connectedness occurs just before she boards the schooner en route to Carriacou. As she observes the throng of out-islanders waiting for the *Emmanuel C,* Avey experiences a familiar sensation, the "same strange sensation" she had felt at events similar to the Carriacou excursion. Memory takes her backward to her family's annual excursion, the boat ride up the Hudson, where as a child she had experienced the same "strange sensation":

> she would feel what seemed to be hundreds of slender threads
> streaming out from her navel and from the place where her heart
> was to enter those around her. And the threads went out not
> only to people she recognized from the neighborhood but to . . .
> the roomers just up from the South [and to] . . . the small group
> of West Indians. . . . The threads streaming out from her even
> entered the few disreputable types . . . from the poolrooms and
> bars. (190)

Soon after Avey recollects these thin, "silken" threads that streamed out from her, she remembers also their essential reciprocal nature. "Then it would seem to her that she had it all wrong, and the threads didn't come from her, but from them, from everyone on the pier . . . issuing out of their navels and hearts to stream into her. . . . While the impression lasted she would cease being herself. . . . She became part of, indeed the center of, a huge wide confraternity" (191). This confraternity, the strange sensation Avey feels on the dock while waiting for the *Emmanuel C*, triggers associations to Tatem, South Carolina, where, with her Great Aunt Cuney, Avey had felt the same sensation as she witnessed the unitive presence in the performance of the ring shout. The recollection extends also to the services at Mount Olivet Baptist Church where the church "mothers" (women whose long service and great age had earned them a title more distinguished than "sister"), "reached out to steady those taken too violently with the spirit . . . the sinners and the back sliders . . . it was their exhortation which helped to bring them through" (194). In this rite of religious communion, the church mothers had helped the members of the congregation to "cross over," to transcend the self in the collective power of unitive spirituality.

In having Avey recollect these rites of communion from the past, Marshall prepares her protagonist for the final participation in the Nation Dance, the ritual of celebratory communion that concludes this novel. When she finally joins in the rhythmic performance of the dance, "an arm made of many arms reached out from the circle to draw her in" (247). The rhythmic shuffle of the Nation Dance that Avey first observes and then participates in, as Barbara Christian notes, is a collective ritual process serving several purposes. It is a ceremony of begging pardon, correct naming, honoring, and celebration.[26] It is the ritual that finally connects Avey to that age-old something she has been missing. Resurrecting and affirming a collective will and purposefulness, the Nation Dance is what enables Avey to finally "cross over" and to endure. As Marshall writes, " . . . in a tumult of voices, drums and ringing iron . . . her feet held to the restrained glide-and-stamp, the rhythmic trudge of the Carriacou tramp, the shuffle designed to stay the course of history" (250).

Because they recapture and affirm an essential life force, a human will and purposefulness that "stays the course of history," celebratory and purgative rites of communion are compulsively reenacted in *The Chosen Place, the Timeless People*. For the epigraph of this novel, Marshall records a saying from the Tiv of West Africa.

> "Once a great wrong has been done, it never dies. People speak
> the words of peace, but their hearts do not forgive. Generations
> perform ceremonies of reconciliation but there is no end."

Victims of time and history, the characters in this novel compulsively tell and listen, enact and reenact rites of communion because the great wrong that has been done to them has become rooted in their unconscious. No longer resolvable by cognitive means, the great wrong can be expurgated only through ritual, through "ceremonies of reconciliation."[27]

Rites of communion in *The Chosen Place* are therefore rites of exorcism, frequently, purgative expressions of entrapment and exploited marginality. At the same time, they are just as frequently collective rites of reconciliation and celebration that heal and renew. In a manner similar to Morrison, Marshall uses these rites to define community, to present character, and finally to develop her thematic inquiry into the notion of what she calls "a common humanity which joins us to humans everywhere."[28]

The episode of the Sunday pig-sticking assists in the development of this theme as it defines and develops Marshall's characterization of Saul Abrams. Rendered through the perceptions of this character, the pig-sticking ritual is presented as a rite of exorcism, a sacrificial rite of communion that effects psychic release for Saul as well as the Spiretown men.

Overcoming his initial squeamishness at the blood, flies, and smells accompanying the ritual, Saul decides to observe the pig-sticking on the Sunday when Leesy's great white sow is butchered. Unduly affected by the resistance to death of this particular animal, a pig to which Delbert ascribes "human feelings," Saul wonders himself "whether something human wasn't being offered upon the battered table." He is moreover puzzled by the cold, methodical, and ruthless way the men dehair the animal. To him their actions suggested "forces at their depth . . . some greater violence," that he had not suspected were there. His impressions are contradictory.

Although he has been just an observer and witness to the animal's death, Saul, when he walks home, not only feels the "profound displacement" of the outsider, but also, he feels strangely thwarted by the inevitability of his outsider status, by the inevitability of his own death, "of being in a house where the shades had already been drawn, the wreath and crepe already hung on the door, and the next of kin . . . simply waiting for the final word" (259). These morbid reflections are soon countered by a strange elation.

> And yet to contradict these impressions he was at the same time strangely elated. . . . In the midst of all the things that had disturbed him about the pig-sticking, there had been beneath the violence of the act an affirmation of something age-old, a sense of renewal, which had left him exhilarated, in a high mood . . . empty but clean inside. (259)

For Saul, the pig-sticking ritual not only affords new insight to universal cycle of life and death, but also a psychic release.

For the Spiretown men, the ritual achieves release of a different kind and by means of a very different process. As Marshall presents it, even through Saul's perceptions and response, the methodical and violent dehairing of the pig for Delbert, Ferguson, and Collins is a purgative expression of frustration and entrapment, an ancient rite of exorcism. Functioning in much the same way as the sacrificial rite of communion in *Sula*, this ancient exorcistic rite is a "necessary stopping point." It is the "moment of rest" that renews and revitalizes an innate sense of life. As a sacrificial rite of communion, the pig-sticking ritual connects these men to the essential, primordial life force and to its power and capacity for endless resurgence.

As the pig-sticking ritual enables Marshall to characterize Saul Abrams and the Spiretown men, rites of communion are used similarly for the characterization of Saul's wife, Harriet. To characterize Harriet as the antithesis of the life force, that timeless will and purposefulness enabling her other characters to endure, Marshall situates Harriet as a part of, but apart from, two central rites of human interaction and connectedness that activate the life force. These two rites of confraternity are the masque of Pyre Hill and the "reckless plunging dance."

As Harriet watches the Bournehills performance of the Pyre Hill masque, she is alternately "moved and disturbed," but she remains apart. The narrator tells us she is "essentially out of it, removed, the spectator looking on." Regarding the masque as a somewhat "busy drama," she dimly understands its meaning. This dim, incomplete understanding of the masque is a consequence of Harriet's equally inadequate understanding of the Bournehills people, whom she sees alternately as a "swollen tide of humanity" and a "huge amoeboid mass." To a large extent, Harriet's response to the performance of the masque foreshadows and precipitates her reaction in the episode of the "reckless plunging dance," the rite of celebratory communion that concludes carnival.

In the episode of the "reckless plunging dance," unitive will and purposefulness flow from and charge the group of young people known as the "guerilla band from the Heights." This green-clad, singing, dancing group comes into being after the performance by the Bournehills band. In their eagerness to "jump with Bournehills," the newly formed collectivity, a throng of adolescents firing noisy toy guns, sweep Harriet Abrams into their midst. Believing that in its recklessness and laughing wrong-headedness, the group would end in the bay, Harriet attempts to direct and advise them. But the group pays no heed. Instead, the adolescents propel themselves forward and continue on their route, "staring with a strange fixity straight ahead, utterly absorbed in what seemed some goal or objective visible only to them" (295). Ignored and insulted, Harriet is stricken by rage, revulsion, and terror. She lashes out. "She swatted away at them the way one would at a swarm of flies, and they as indifferent to her blows as they had been to her insistent voice before, continued to sing and fire the guns and perform the reckless plunging dance" (296).

In terms of Harriet's characterization and the structure of the novel, what is important here is that the writer presents the episode from two perspectives: the narrator's and Harriet's. The narrator's perspective, which is clearly presented, is that these adolescents are enacting a rite of celebratory communion, magnifying carnival. For Harriet, however, this celebratory rite is a "reckless plunging dance" and a nightmare. But the nightmare is Harriet's and hers alone. For the throng of adolescents does not spill headlong into the bay as she had feared, but skillfully moves, a few at a time, to avoid the water and to reach the sports oval just beyond the town—the goal that had been visible only to them. Though Harriet is swept along with the group, she is clearly apart from it and its celebratory unitive presence; she is therefore unaware of the goal.

She is keenly aware, however, of their collective will and purpose-fulness, "the thing that she had seen in their eyes." Confronted by a unitive will that effectively thwarts her own, self-destructive will to dominate, Harriet suffers psychic demise during the "reckless plunging dance." She is left "victim," the narrator tells us, of "some casual crucifixion."

In terms of the structure of the novel, Harriet's psychic death at carnival foreshadows her suicide. Her perspective on carnival and her perception of its celebrants as a "huge amoeboid mass," prevent her from understanding its essential nature as a "huge, wide human confraternity." Because she does not understand, she cannot connect to these fundamentally human rites. Separate and apart from these rites that activate the life force and collective, unitive will, Harriet succumbs to her own self-destructive will and takes her life.

For the people of Bournehills, this collective will and purpose-fulness are activated in the ritualistic performance of the masque of Cuffee Ned and Pyre Hill. Performed annually at carnival, the masque affirms their ability as human beings to transcend place, time, and themselves. It is this transcendence in the power of their collective history that enables them to resist, suffer, and endure.

Regarded by the crowd as the "same foolishness" that spoiled every carnival, the Pyre Hill masque is initially a counterpoint to the gaiety of the carnival. It tells a story the crowd already knows and prefers not to see or hear again. Undaunted, the Bournehills contingent sings, enacts, and relives the saga: the long march, the stern exile, the rebellion, the death of Cuffee Ned, their shaman, seer, and obeah man. And because they must tell the whole story, they sing also of the bloody suppression that followed. By the time of its completion, the performance has the entire town on its shoulders and "reeling at its base." The affective presence generated by the Bournehills masque, Marshall tells us, derives from the "truth" it contains, the truth of universal suffering.

> Yet as those fused voices continued to mount the air . . . it didn't seem they were singing only of themselves and Bournehills, but of people like them everywhere . . . [of] the experience through which any people who find themselves ill-used, dispossessed, at the mercy of the powerful, must pass. (286–87)

The seminal achievement of the Bournehills people, the performers sing, had been the creation of a maroon community. Free, at peace, and independent, this community had lasted for nearly three years— in communion with the gods, its members in communion with each other. *"They had worked together.* . . . Under Cuffee, they sang, a man had not lived for himself alone, but for his neighbor also. 'If we had lived selfish, we couldn't have lived at all.' . . . They had trusted one another, had set aside their differences and stood as one against their enemies. *They had been a people"* (287). Through the representation of purgative and celebratory rites of communion in a specific time and place, the "chosen" Caribbean isle of Bournehills and its "timeless" people, Marshall gives aesthetic form to her notion of "collective humanity."

Rites of communion in Marshall's and Morrison's fiction, and the actualization of communion in Saar's and Ringgold's multimedia and performance art give form to a certain, vital aesthetic concern. The human need for ritual and the regenerative power of human connectedness in ritual constitute its essence and source. Collectively, these artists appropriate the essential feature of reciprocity from folk performance to replicate and represent the power and sense of communion. As realized in their works, communion is the sign of continuity, of the unyielding human will to stay the course of history. It is finally the sign of the human capacity for transformation and regeneration through ritual.

In representing human connectedness through ritual in their art, Morrison, Marshall, Ringgold, and Saar engage an aesthetic of functional form. In the preceding chapters, I have traced the relationship between that aesthetic and vernacular folk culture. With the first chapter establishing how engagement with the identity issues of the 1960s generated certain attitudes and ideas about black folklore, subsequent chapters delineate the expression of those ideas in the art these women produced during the following two decades. Chapter 2, "Folk Magic, Women, and Identity," explores how they transgressed the borders of patriarchist black nationalism to frame a womanist intervention. Sacralizing the experience of mothering, nurturing, and healing, they reclaim folk magic and its female practitioners to legitimate discredited forms of knowledge.

The aesthetic return to and re-creation of Africa and its centrality to production of a functional, cultural identity is the focus of Chapter 3, which charts the journey of return in fiction and the use of materials and symbols reflecting *Africanité* in art. Finally, the fourth chapter delineates how performative elements from black folk culture are appropriated by each of these artists, to represent and replicate the "sense of communion," to actualize an aesthetic of conjunctive duality, and to address the degree to which a work of art is equally constructed by artist and viewer.

On the cover of a recent issue of the *International Review of African American Art*, a new work by Betye Saar, *The Liberation of Aunt Jemima: Busy Bee* (1997) appears above the title for the issue: "Stereotypes: Subverted or For Sale?" Articles and interviews inside the issue address the new national conversation on race and the intense debate on the artistic use of racial stereotypes and derogatory images. While what I have sought to do in this book, to some degree, contextualizes that debate, the intent of this study has been to contextualize art, black women's art in particular, and to map the aesthetic sensibilities of the artists selected for this study: Betye Saar, Faith Ringgold, Toni Morrison, and Paule Marshall. Using the 1960s cultural revolution in the United States as a point of departure, what I found was that the "fecundating matrix" of black folklore, as Toni Cade Bambara called it, was the mechanism through which these women transgressed borders and translated their own multiple, shifting, and heterogenous identities. It may be useful to consider that even in this postmodernist era of the 1990s, with its aesthetics of pastiche, parody, and possibility, that same "fecundating matrix" remains a viable strategy for border crossing and a substantive base for art.

NOTES

INTRODUCTION

1. Gloria Anzaldúa, *Borderlands/La Frontera: The New Mestiza*, preface, 3; Carole Boyce Davies, *Black Women, Writing, and Identity: Migrations of the Subject*, 66–67.

2. Richard Bauman, "Folklore," in *Folklore, Cultural Performances, and Popular Entertainments: A Communications-Centered Handbook*, 40; Zora Neale Hurston quoted in Barbara Johnson, *A World of Difference*, 160.

3. Dan Ben-Amos, "Toward A Definition of Folklore in Context," 5, 14.

4. Patricia Hill Collins, *Black Feminist Thought: Knowledge, Consciousness, and the Politics of Empowerment*, 201–3.

5. I derive the notion of conjunctive duality from Theophus H. Smith, *Conjuring Culture: Biblical Formations of Black America*, 142–45.

6. Henry A. Giroux, *Border Crossings: Cultural Workers and the Politics of Education*, 169.

7. Giroux, *Border Crossings*, 232.

8. Davies, *Black Women, Writing, and Identity*, 119; Edward Brathwaite quoted on 191n.

1. FOLKLORE AND THE BORDERLAND OF THE SIXTIES

1. Kathleen M. Ashley, ed., *Victor Turner and the Construction of Cultural Criticism*, xviii. For discussions of borders, borderlands, and

identity, see Giroux, *Border Crossings;* and Anzaldúa, *Borderlands/La Frontera.*

2. Paul Gilroy, "Roots and Routes: Black Identity as an Outernational Project," 19; Lucy Lippard, *Mixed Blessings: New Art in a Multicultural America,* 12; Nancy Hartsock, "Rethinking Modernism: Minority vs. Majority Theories," 26; Henry Louis Gates Jr., "The Master's Pieces: On Canon Formation and the African American Tradition," 105.

3. I derive this definition of cultural identity from Stuart Hall, "Cultural Identity and Diaspora."

4. Paul Gilroy, *The Black Atlantic: Modernity and Double Consciousness,* 219. Gilroy makes this observation in his discussion of Toni Morrison's *Beloved.*

5. Madhu Dubey, *Black Women Novelists and the Nationalist Aesthetic,* 17.

6. Gwen Bergner, "The Role of Gender in Fanon's *Black Skin, White Masks,*" 87.

7. Toni Cade Bambara, ed., *The Black Woman: An Anthology,* 8.

8. Dubey, *Black Women Novelists,* 13.

9. Art historians and critics have described three themes in the work Saar produced during the late 1960s and 1970s: magic/occult, black liberation, and reclamation of past time. See Larry Rosing, "Betye Saar"; and Arna Alexander Bontemps, Jacqueline Fonvielle-Bontemps, and David Driskell, *Forever Free: Art by African American Women, 1862–1980,* 122.

10. Andrea Liss, "Power and Gentle Force."

11. Lynn F. Miller and Sally Swenson, "Betye Saar," 179.

12. Paule Marshall, "Shaping the World of My Art," 103, 105.

13. Mary Helen Washington, "I Sign My Mother's Name: Alice Walker, Dorothy West, Paule Marshall," 164, 165.

14. "Runagate" is the title of a poem by Robert Hayden that accentuates the slave past and fugitive escape from bondage. It is also the title of part 1 of Marshall's *Praisesong for the Widow* and the folk expression for "renegade." "Lavé Tête," the title of part 3 of *Praisesong,* refers to the voodoo ceremony of "washing clean" or "washing the head" (Leslie G. Desmangles, *The Faces of the Gods: Vodou and Roman Catholicism in Haiti,* 87). Marshall, "Shaping the World of My Art," 106.

15. Mary Helen Washington, ed., *Midnight Birds: Stories of Contemporary Black Women Writers*, 43; Eugenia Collier, "The Closing of the Circle: Movement from Division to Wholeness in Paule Marshall's Fiction"; see also Joyce Pettis, *Toward Wholeness in Paule Marshall's Fiction*. The political perspective in Marshall's work may be linked also to her association, during the 1950s and 1960s, with the American Youth for Democracy and Artists for Freedom. In 1964, she participated in the historic symposium, "The Black Revolution and the White Backlash." Marshall, "Shaping the World of My Art," 103.

16. Marshall, "Shaping the World of My Art," 107, 108.

17. Toni Morrison, "Rootedness: The Ancestor as Foundation," 339.

18. Susan Willis, "Eruptions of Funk: Historicizing Toni Morrison," 269.

19. Toni Morrison, "City Limits, Village Values: Concepts of Neighborhood in Black Fiction," 43; Morrison, "Rootedness," 344.

20. Claudia Tate, ed., "Toni Morrison," in *Black Women Writers at Work*, 129.

21. Morrison, "City Limits," 43.

22. Gloria Naylor, "'A Conversation': Toni Morrison and Gloria Naylor," 577; Rosemarie K. Lester, "An Interview with Toni Morrison, Hessian Radio Network, Frankfurt, West Germany," in Nellie McKay, ed., *Critical Essays on Toni Morrison*, 52; Toni Morrison, "Rediscovering Black History," 22. As with the preceding comment, this statement represents Morrison's retrospective analysis of her attitudes and perceptions during the sixties.

23. Robert B. Stepto, "'Intimate Things in Place': An Interview with Toni Morrison," 474.

24. Ibid., 474; Morrison, "Rediscovering Black History," 16. The latter quotation is also in "A Slow Walk of Trees (as Grandmother Would Say) Hopeless (as Grandfather Would Say)," 156.

25. Matt Damsker, "Performance Creates a Tableau," 1–2.

26. Terrie Rouse, "Faith Ringgold—A Mirror of Her Community," 10.

27. Borgatti quoted in Frieda High-Wasikhongo, "Afrofemcentric: Twenty Years of Faith Ringgold," 18.

28. Rouse, "Faith Ringgold—A Mirror," 10; Thalia Gouma-Peterson, "Faith Ringgold's Narrative Quilts," 9.

29. Eleanor Munro, "Who's Afraid of Aunt Jemima: History and Style," 21.

30. Henry Louis Gates Jr., *Figures in Black: Words, Signs, and the "Racial" Self*. Gates uses the word *context* to refer to the "textual" world that a black text echoes, revises, and responds to in various formal ways. For my own term, *critical-aesthetic context*, I use and expand Gates's definition to include visual art as well as borrow his phrasing to explain the term.

31. Mae G. Henderson, ed., *Borders, Boundaries, and Frames: Essays in Cultural Criticism and Cultural Studies*, 3.

32. Bontemps et al., *Forever Free*, 39.

33. Lerone Bennett Jr., introduction to *Tradition and Conflict: Images of a Turbulent Decade, 1963–1973*, 9.

34. Abiola Irele, "Négritude or Black Cultural Nationalism," 321.

35. Harold Cruse, *The Crisis of the Negro Intellectual*, 337–44; 533–43. For his analysis and succinct phrasing of Cruse's view of black nationalism, I am indebted to Donn Granville Davis, "Image • Symbol Control and the Black Arts: A Tentative Note on the Need for Organization," 34.

36. Africobra was organized after the Chicago mural project, circa 1968, as COBRA (Coalition of Black Revolutionary Artists) and later became AFRI-COBRA, which developed three exhibitions between 1968 and 1973; OBAC (Organization of Black American Culture) included a literary workshop under the aegis of Hoyt Fuller and a visual art workshop headed by William Walker and Jeff Donaldson; the poet-critic Larry Neal and LeRoi Jones were the major spokesmen for the Black Arts Movement and coeditors of the anthology *Black Fire* (1968), which reflected the tenets of the movement. Jones, who later became Amiri Baraka, established the Black Arts Theatre in 1965. Forum 66 was a Detroit-based black cultural organization formed around the same generalized aesthetic-critical theories of cultural nationalism and the Black Aesthetic. AMSAC, the American Society for African Culture, based in New York, provided the most direct link with African proponents of Négritude, Leopold Senghor and Aime Cesaire especially. See Mary Schmidt Campbell's work in *Tradition and Conflict: Images of a Turbulent Decade*. See also David Lionel Smith, "Chicago Poets, OBAC, and the Black Arts Movement," in Werner Sollors and Maria Diedrich, eds., *The Black*

Columbiad: Defining Moments in African American Literature and Culture, 253–64.

37. Larry Neal, "The Black Arts Movement," 257–61.

38. Lee Ransaw, "The Changing Relationship of the Black Visual Artist to His Community," 49.

39. Hoyt Fuller, "The New Black Literature: Protest or Affirmation," 327.

40. Addison Gayle Jr., introduction to *The Way of the New World*, reprinted in Richard A. Long and Eugenia Collier, eds., *Afro-American Writing: An Anthology*, 661.

41. Davis, "Image • Symbol Control," 33; Charles Johnson, *Being and Race: Black Writing since 1970*, 17–18. Johnson's discussion centers on the concept of guarding the image and image control, during the Harlem Renaissance and later, as an attempt to control meaning.

42. Davis, "Image • Symbol Control," 34.

43. Ibid.

44. Quoted in Archie Epps, ed., *The Speeches of Malcolm X at Harvard*, 142.

45. Members of the Atlanta Project of the Student Non-violent Coordinating Committee, "A Position Paper on Race," in Joanne Grant, ed., *Black Protest: History, Documents, and Analyses, 1619 to the Present*, 452–56.

46. Partly because of its permutations from aesthetic philosophy to political doctrine, Négritude is a concept not easily defined. Janheinz Jahn in *Neo-African Literature* does a good job of summarizing the several meanings. Jacques Louis Hyman's *Leopold Sedar Senghor: An Intellectual Biography* gives a detailed account of the origins and philosophical bases of the doctrine.

47. Cheikh Anta Diop, *The African Origin of Civilization: Myth or Reality*, 27n; Richard Long has used the term *ancestralism* to describe Locke's theory of cultural identification with Africa and has included the essay in *Afro-American Writing*, 303–304.

48. Cruse, *Crisis of the Negro Intellectual*, 421.

49. Campbell, "A Turbulent Decade," in *Tradition and Conflict*, 59.

50. Leslie King Hammond, *Ritual and Myth: A Survey of African American Art, June 20, 1982–November 1, 1982*, 11–12.

51. David Driskell, introduction to Hammond, *Ritual and Myth*, 7.

52. Bontemps et al., *Forever Free*, 39.

53. Audre Lorde, "Learning from the Sixties," 136.

54. Morrison, "Rediscovering Black History," 14; Lynn F. Miller and Sally Swenson, "Faith Ringgold," 168.

55. Morrison, "Rediscovering Black History," 14.

56. Carolyn Fowler, *Black Arts and Black Aesthetics*, xxiv. Recent work by the young African American artist Kara Walker has generated new discussion on the artistic use of derogatory images, a discussion in which Betye Saar is much involved. In addition to a symposium at Hammonds House Galleries in Atlanta, one at Harvard in March 1998, the *International Review of African American Art*, vol. 14, no. 3, addresses the subject.

57. Fredric Jameson, *The Political Unconscious: Narrative as a Socially Symbolic Act*, 79.

58. Campbell, "A Turbulent Decade," in *Tradition and Conflict*, 47, 60.

59. Houston Baker, *Blues, Ideology, and Afro-American Literature: A Vernacular Theory*, 3. Baker conceptualized the blues as matrix and mediational site. I appropriate both to African American folkloric forms and modify Baker's phrasing.

2. FOLK MAGIC, WOMEN, AND IDENTITY

1. George McCall, "Symbiosis: The Case of Hoodoo and the Numbers Racket," 420. At one point, the view that folk magic represented continuity with Africa was controversial. While there were folklorists who held that conjure and other forms of folk magic were African in origin, there were those who argued its European provenance. For a recent, concise summary of the controversy, see Isidore Okpewho, "The Cousins of Uncle Remus," in Sollors and Diedrich, eds., *Black Columbiad*.

2. Zora Neale Hurston, *Mules and Men*, 193–251; Ruth Bass, "Mojo"; Leonora Herron and Alice M. Bacon, "Conjuring and Conjure-Doctors"; McCall, "Symbiosis," 420.

3. Marjorie Pryse, "Zora Neale Hurston, Alice Walker, and the 'Ancient Power' of Black Women"; Gouma-Peterson, "Faith Ringgold's Narrative Quilts," 10. *Mojo* and *gris-gris* refer to the paraphernalia used in folk magic as well as to the process itself. Eleanor Munro, "Betye Saar," 259.

4. Jean Strouse, "Toni Morrison's Black Magic," 54; Trinh T. Minh-ha, *Woman, Native, Other: Writing Postcoloniality and Feminism*, 129; I appropriate *sacralize* from Hans Mol, *Identity and the Sacred*, 1–5.

5. Alan Dundes, ed., *Mother Wit from the Laughing Barrel: Readings in the Interpretation of Afro-American Folklore*, 357; see also Henry Mitchell, *Black Belief: Folk Beliefs of Blacks in America and West Africa*, 23; Hurston, *Mules and Men*, 193.

6. Henry Mitchell, *Black Belief*, 27, 55–56; Smith, *Conjuring Culture*, 18.

7. Jones, "Changing Same," 113; Addison Gayle Jr.'s *The Black Aesthetic* contains valuable information on this topic. For additional discussion on the "spiritual reference" for art by black Americans, see Ron Wellburn, "The Black Aesthetic Imperative"; in the same volume, see also LeRoi Jones, "The Changing Same (R&B and New Black Music)," 113; Larry Neal, "Black Arts Movement"; Ishmael Reed, "Can a Metronome Know the Thunder or Summon a God?"; and Sarah Webster Fabio, "Tripping with Black Writing."

8. Reed, "Can a Metronome Know?" 381.

9. Houston Conwill, "An Interview with Betye Saar," 9.

10. Peter Clothier, *Betye Saar*, 24. *Nommo* refers to the power of naming in African religious thought. Defined by Janheinz Jahn as "the vital force that carries the word," Nommo is a spiritual-physical unity or fluidity which flows into humans from the collective spirits of the ancestors and of God. Activated by speech, song, and incantation, nommo accompanies all human activity, especially acts of creation: from conception and birth, to art, to practices of magic. See Janheinz Jahn, *Muntu: An Outline of New African Culture*, 121–55.

11. Clothier, *Betye Saar*, 24–25.

12. Minh-ha, *Woman, Native, Other*, 128.

13. Robert Farris Thompson, *African Art in Motion*, 99–107; Dominique Zahan, *The Religion, Spirituality, and Thought of Traditional Africa*, 83–84.

14. Giroux, *Border Crossings*, 138.

15. Clothier, *Betye Saar*, 11.

16. Ibid.

17. Eleanor Munro, "Faith Ringgold," 416; Marjorie Halpin, "Confronting the Looking-Glass Men: A Preliminary Examination of the Mask."

18. Marshall, *Praisesong for the Widow*, 107; all subsequent references are to the 1984 Dutton edition and will appear in the text.

19. Karla F. C. Holloway, "On Morrison and Black Female Memory," 151, 152.

20. Paule Marshall, *The Chosen Place, The Timeless People*, 27; all subsequent references are to the 1984 Vintage edition and will appear in the text.

21. Toni Morrison, *Sula*, 126; all subsequent references are to the 1973 Alfred Knopf edition and will appear in the text.

22. Toni Morrison, *Song of Solomon*; all subsequent references are to the 1977 Alfred Knopf edition and will appear in the text.

23. "Spirit Catcher: The Art of Betye Saar," television interview, *The Originals: Women in Art Series*, WNET, New York, 1978. Suzanne Bauman was the interviewer. Saar has described her creative ritual in print: "It includes the following stages and/or procedures: 1) The imprint—ideas, thoughts, memories, dreams from the past, present and future. 2) The search—the selective eye and intuition. 3) The collecting, gathering, and accumulating of objects and materials, each bringing a presence, an energy (old, new, ethnic, organic). 4) The recycling and transformation—the materials and objects are manipulated and combined with various media (paint, chalk, glue). The energy is integrated and expanded. 5) The release—the work is shared (exhibited), experienced, and relinquished. The 'ritual' completed." See Mary Schmidt Campbell, *Rituals: The Art of Betye Saar*.

24. Mol, *Identity and the Sacred*, 1–15, 202; Carole D. Yawney, "Dread Wasteland: Rastafarian Ritual."

25. Carole Boyce Davies, "Mothering and Healing in Recent Black Women's Fiction."

26. Barbara Christian, "Ritualistic Process and the Structure of Paule Marshall's *Praisesong for the Widow*," 74.

27. Stephanie Demetrakopoulos, "Morrison's Literary and Cultural Contributions: Originality and Richness," in Holloway and Demetrakopoulos, eds., *New Dimensions of Spirituality*, 161.

3. RECLAIMING AND RE-CREATING AFRICA
Folklore and the "Return to the Source"

1. Davies, *Black Women, Writing, and Identity*, 10. Davies asserts that Africa as homeland countermanded European deployment of its

reality and the attempt to redefine identities for others. For reference to yearning as a mechanism for connection, see bell hooks, *Yearning: Race, Gender, and Cultural Politics*, 113.

2. Saar expresses her belief about African influences and folk art in several interviews; see Harriett P. Marcus, "Once More with Feeling: The Art of Betye Saar"; Crystal Britton, "Betye Saar"; and Catherine Fox, "The Artist as Shaman: The Ordinary Becomes Special with Betye Saar."

3. Trudier Harris, *Exorcising Blackness: Historical and Literary Lynching and Burning Rituals*, 2; Harris quotes Walter White on page 7 of the same work.

4. Fox, "Artist as Shaman"; Susan Pettit, "Saar Explores Interior Space"; Robert Goldwater, "The Western Experience of Negro Art." On a number of occasions, Saar has acknowledged the influence of the Watts Towers on her development as an artist. One hundred feet high, the towers are a mosaic of broken bottles, mirrors, dishes, shells, and rocks, described by Peter Clothier as the "detritus of a civilization recycled into one of its finest cultural monuments." See Clothier, *Betye Saar*, 30.

5. Kip Lornell, *"Happy in the Service of the Lord": African American Sacred Vocal Harmony Quartets in Memphis*, 2–3; Eric Lott, *Love and Theft: Blackface Minstrelsy and the American Working Class*, 8; Ralph Ellison, "Change the Joke and Slip the Yoke," 58, 59.

6. Judith Wragg Chase, *Afro-American Art and Craft*, 52–57.

7. Miller and Swenson, "Faith Ringgold," 161.

8. Zahan, *Religion, Spirituality, and Thought*, 83–84.

9. Dundes, ed., *Mother Wit*, 523; Grace Glueck, "An Artist Who Turns Cloth into Social Commentary." According to Dundes, *memorate* is a technical folkloristic term intended to designate narratives related by individuals about a purely personal experience of their own. A "family memorate," then, relates a personal family experience.

10. Grace Glueck, "An Artist Who Turns Cloth into Social Commentary," 25; Faith Ringgold, "Who's Afraid of Aunt Jemima?: A Book of Story Quilts and Personal Narrative on the Life of Faith Ringgold," 5. Ringgold's written commentary explaining the genesis of the quilt was provided by the Bernice Steinbaum Gallery, Ltd., N.Y.

11. Gouma-Peterson, "Faith Ringgold's Narrative Quilts," 8. Gouma-Peterson's reference to these characteristics of the dilemma tale, while drawn from another source, are supported by William R. Bascom, *African Dilemma Tales*.

12. For more in this work, see the "Bitter Nest Series," in *Faith Ringgold: A Twenty-five Year Survey: April 1 to June 24, 1990*, 41–45.

13. For a description of African pattern-dyed and woven textile techniques, see Maude Wahlman, *Contemporary African Arts*, 12–25; Sally Price and Richard Price, *Afro-American Arts of the Suriname Rain Forest*, 60–80; and Chase, *Afro-American Art and Craft*, 87–89.

14. *With Fingers of Love: Economic Development and the Civil Rights Movement.*

15. For a discussion of these elements in African and African American aesthetics, see Wadsworth A. Jarrell, "Heading for a Black Aesthetic," 17–18; and Roger D. Abrahams's introduction to his *African Folktales: Traditional Stories of the Black World*, 6–8.

16. Faith Ringgold, "Women's Traditional Art."

17. Elsie Clews Parsons, *Folklore of the Antilles, French and English*, 48–52.

18. Joanna Cole, *Best Loved Folktales*, 668.

19. Robert J. O'Meally, "Tar Baby, She Don't Say Nothin'," 197. O'Meally references Morrison's introductory comments for the Franklin edition of the novel.

20. Karla F. C. Holloway, "African Values and Western Chaos."

21. Morrison, *Tar Baby*, 206; all subsequent references are to the 1981 Alfred Knopf edition and will appear in the text.

22. Maroon communities were communities created by escaped slaves or never-enslaved Africans. They were concomitant with plantation slavery in the Americas and ranged from small bands that survived for a few months to powerful states with thousands of members that survived for centuries. For a brief history of the Suriname Maroons in South America, see Price and Price, *Afro-American Arts*, 14–15. For reference to maroon communities in the United States, see Angela Davis, "Reflections on the Black Woman's Role in the Community of Slaves."

23. Wilfred G. O. Cartey, "Africa of My Grandmother Singing: Curving Rhythms," 10.

24. Holloway, "African Values," 121. While Holloway sees the

night women as offering the opportunity to recall and reconnect with "racial memory," my view is that these women offer symbolic nurturance as well.

25. Thomas Le Clair, "A Conversation with Toni Morrison: 'The Language Must Not Sweat,'" 27.

26. Angelita Reyes, "Ancient Properties of the New World: The Paradox of the 'Other' in Toni Morrison's *Tar Baby*," 25.

27. O'Meally, "Tar Baby," 197.

28. Christian, "Ritualistic Process," 78. Like Holloway's reading of *Tar Baby*, Christian's reading of this novel coincides with my own.

29. John Williams, trans., "Return of a Native Daughter: An Interview with Paule Marshall and Maryse Conde," 52.

30. Savannah Unit of the Georgia Writers' Project, *Drums and Shadows: Survival Studies among the Georgia Coastal Negroes*, 65–72 (hereafter referred to as *Drums and Shadows*). Ibo Landing on St. Simon's Island is referenced also in *Drums and Shadows*.

31. Christian, "Ritualistic Process," 76; see also Virginia Hamilton, *The People Could Fly: American Black Folktales*; Hamilton explains that there are numerous tales exemplifying this "wish-fulfillment motif" in black American folklore.

32. Christian, "Ritualistic Process," 76.

33. Zahan, *Religion, Spirituality, and Thought*, 89, 47.

34. Christian, "Ritualistic Process," 79.

35. Ibid., 83.

4. FOLKLORE AS PERFORMANCE AND COMMUNION

1. The phrase "sense of communion" is part of Leopold Sedar Senghor's concept of Négritude; see Ali A. Mazrui, *Cultural Forces in World Politics*, 134–35; and Irving Leonard Markovitz, *Leopold Sedar Senghor and the Politics of Négritude*, 41. Tom F. Driver, *Liberating Rites: Understanding the Transformative Power of Ritual*, xii–xviii.

2. In his discussion of African masks, Segy references this concept of harmonizing as essentially the same as that informing the ritual of communion. See Ladislas Segy, *Masks of Black Africa*, 18.

3. Françoise Lionnet, *Postcolonial Representations: Women, Literature, Identity*, 5–6.

4. Melville Herskovits, *The Myth of the Negro Past*, 152.

5. Stephen Henderson, *Understanding the New Black Poetry*, 30–31.

6. Pearl Williams-Jones, "Performance Style in Black Gospel Music," 118.

7. Damsker, "Performance Creates a Tableau," 1; see also Laura Stewart Dishman, "Ringgold Uses Fabric as a Thread to Her Past"; Conwill, "Interview with Betye Saar," 10.

8. I refer to Ringgold's *No Name Performance II*, described later in this chapter, and to *Wake and Resurrection* and *The Bitter Nest*, discussed in Chapter 3. Contemporary black rhythm and blues, African cosmological beliefs, African textile techniques, and the Harlem Renaissance of the 1920s constitute the cultural and ideological context for these works. Mojo charms, fetishes, and other references to voodoo constitute a similar context for Saar's work. While it is tempting to speculate that Ringgold's performance pieces and Saar's cumulative-participatory art events reflect the influence of European and American performance-art movements like Fluxus, Aktionismus, Living Art, and Body Art, Faith Ringgold in her memoirs categorically denies that she was influenced by them. Performance in those movements, through the experience and confirmation of one's "own self" in its temporal, spatial, and/or corporeal dimension, attempted to establish communication and interaction with the "other person," to achieve, affirm, and celebrate a transcendent "we" identity. I will hypothesize, still, that the affective-participatory relationship between audience and performance characterizing black performance offered both Saar and Ringgold the opportunity to affirm cultural identity and, at the same time, link their work to contemporaneous art-world notions of performance.

9. Paule Marshall, "From the Poet's Kitchen," 28; Marshall, "Shaping the World of My Art," 105; Tate, "Toni Morrison," in *Black Women Writers at Work*, 125.

10. Morrison, "Rootedness," 341.

11. LeRoi Jones, *Blues People: The Negro Experience in White America and the Music that Developed from It*, 26–27; Ron [Maulana] Karenga, "Black Cultural Nationalism," in Gayle, ed., *Black Aesthetic*, 35.

12. See Mazrui, *Cultural Forces*, 209; this phrase is also translated in Markovitz, *Leopold Sedar Senghor*, 41: "In other terms, the sense of communion, the gift of imagination, the gift of rhythm—these are the traits of Négritude, that we find like an indelible seal on all the

works and activities of the black man." For further discussion of Senghor's "sense of communion," see Leopold Senghor, *The Foundations of Africanité, or Négritude and Arabité;* and Senghor, "Négritude: A Humanism of the Twentieth Century."

13. Grace Glueck, "Betye Saar, Artist Inspired by the Occult"; Conwill, "Interview with Betye Saar," 13.

14. See Glueck, "Art: Betye Saar Gives Spirits Form"; and Clothier, *Betye Saar*, 35.

15. Campbell, *Rituals.*

16. Betye Saar, "Installation as Sculpture," 44.

17. Clothier, *Betye Saar*, 36.

18. Damsker, "Performance Creates a Tableau," 1.

19. Michael James, "Beyond the Tradition: The Art of the Studio Quilt," 18.

20. Munro, "Who's Afraid of Aunt Jemima?" 21.

21. Gregory Galligan, "The Quilts of Faith Ringgold," 63.

22. Dishman, "Ringgold Uses Fabric."

23. For this perspective on Suicide Day, I am indebted to Susan Blake's critical article, "Toni Morrison," in *Dictionary of Literary Biography.*

24. Morrison, "Rootedness," 343–44.

25. Cartey, "Africa of My Grandmother's Singing," 11; Jahn, *Muntu*, 11; Zahan, *Religion, Spirituality, and Thought*, 47.

26. Christian, "Ritualistic Process," 82.

27. Winifred L. Stoelting, "Time Past and Time Present: The Search for Viable Links in *The Chosen Place, The Timeless People* by Paule Marshall," 61.

28. Paule Marshall, "The Negro Woman in American Literature," 24.

SELECTED BIBLIOGRAPHY

Abrahams, Roger D. *African Folktales: Traditional Stories of the Black World*. New York: Pantheon, 1983.

——. *Afro-American Folktales: Stories from the Black Tradition in the New World*. New York: Pantheon, 1985.

Andrews, Benny. "Jemimas, Mysticism, and Mojos: The Art of Betye Saar." *Encore American and Worldwide News*, March 17, 1975.

Anzaldúa, Gloria. *Borderlands/La Frontera: The New Mestiza*. San Francisco: Aunt Lute, 1987.

Ashley, Kathleen, M., ed. *Victor Turner and the Construction of Cultural Criticism*. Bloomington: Indiana University Press, 1990.

Ba, Sylvia Washington. *The Concept of Négritude in the Poetry of Leopold Sedar Senghor*. Princeton: Princeton University Press, 1973.

Baker, Houston. *Blues, Ideology, and Afro-American Literature: A Vernacular Theory*. Chicago: University of Chicago Press, 1984.

Bambara, Toni Cade. *Deep Sightings and Rescue Missions: Fiction, Essays, and Conversations*. New York: Pantheon, 1996.

Bambara, Toni Cade, ed. *The Black Woman: An Anthology*. New York: New American Library, 1970.

Banyiwa-Horne, Naana. "The Scary Face of the Self: An Analysis of the Character of Sula in Toni Morrison's *Sula*." *Sage* 1 (spring 1985): 28–31.

Bascom, William R. *African Dilemma Tales*. Chicago: Aldine Publishing, 1975.

————. *Ifa Divination: Communication between Gods and Man in West Africa.* Bloomington: Indiana University Press, 1969.

Bass, Ruth. "Mojo." In *Mother Wit from the Laughing Barrel: Readings in the Interpretation of Afro-American Folklore,* ed. Alan Dundes, 380–87. Englewood Cliffs, N.J.: Prentice Hall, 1973.

Bauman, Richard, ed. *Folklore, Cultural Performances, and Popular Entertainments: A Communications-Centered Handbook.* New York: Oxford University Press, 1992.

Bearing Witness: Contemporary Works by African American Women Artists. New York: Spelman College and Rizzoli International Publications, 1996.

Ben-Amos, Dan. "Toward a Definition of Folklore in Context." In *Toward New Perspectives in Folklore,* ed. Americo Paredes and Richard Bauman, 3–15. Austin: University of Texas Press, 1972.

Ben-Amos, Dan, ed. *Folklore Genres.* Austin: University of Texas Press, 1976.

Bennett, Lerone, Jr. Introduction to *Tradition and Conflict: Images of a Turbulent Decade, 1963–1973.* New York: Studio Museum in Harlem, 1985.

Bergner, Gwen. "The Role of Gender in Fanon's *Black Skin, White Masks.*" *PMLA* 1 (January 1995): 75–87.

Betye Saar. Los Angeles: Museum of Contemporary Art, Los Angeles, 1984.

Betye Saar: Collages. New York: Gallery 62 and The National Urban League, 1979.

Betye Saar: Personal Icons. ExhibitsUSA and Mid-America Arts Alliance, 1995.

Black Art—Ancestral Legacy: The African Impulse in African-American Art. Dallas: Dallas Museum of Art, 1989.

Blake, Susan. "Toni Morrison." In *Afro-American Fiction Writers after 1955,* ed. Thadious M. Davis and Trudier Harris. 187–99. Vol. 33 of *Dictionary of Literary Biography.* Detroit: Gale Research, 1984.

Bontemps, Arna Alexander, Jacqueline Fonvielle-Bontemps, and David Driskell, eds. *Forever Free: Art by African American Women, 1862–1980.* Alexandria, Va.: Stephenson; in association with the Center for the Visual Arts Gallery, Illinois State University, 1980.

Britton, Crystal. "Betye Saar." *Art Papers* 3 (May–June 1984): 4.

Broderick, Francis, and August Meier, eds. *Negro Protest Thought in the Twentieth Century.* New York: Bobbs-Merrill, 1965.

Broude, Norma, and Mary Garrard. *The Power of Feminist Art: The American Movement of the 1970s, History and Impact.* New York: Harry N. Abrams, 1994.

Brown, Doris. "Social Comment Rings True." *New Brunswick (N.J.) Home News,* March 4, 1973, C21.

Campbell, Mary Schmidt. *Rituals: The Art of Betye Saar.* New York: Studio Museum in Harlem, 1980.

————. Foreword to *Tradition and Conflict: Images of a Turbulent Decade, 1963–1973.* New York: Studio Museum in Harlem, 1985.

Cartey, Wilfred G. O. "Africa of My Grandmother Singing: Curving Rhythms." In *Black African Voices,* ed. James E. Miller, Robert O'Neal, and Helen McDonnell, 9–14. Glenview, Ill.: Scott, Foresman, 1970.

Chafe, William. *Civilities and Civil Rights: Greensboro, North Carolina, and the Black Struggle for Freedom.* Oxford: Oxford University Press, 1980.

Chamberlain, Mary, ed. *Writing Lives: Conversations between Women Writers.* London: Virago Press, 1988.

Chase, Judith Wragg. *Afro-American Art and Craft.* New York: Van Nostrand Reinhold, 1971.

Chinosole. "Audre Lorde and Matrilineal Diaspora: 'Moving History beyond Nightmare into Structures for the Future. . . .'" In *Wild Women in the Whirlwind: Culture and Politics of Renaissance Afra-American Writing,* ed. Andrée McLaughlin and J. Braxton, 379–93. New Brunswick: Rutgers University Press, 1990.

Christian, Barbara. "Ritualistic Process and the Structure of Paule Marshall's *Praisesong for the Widow.*" *Callaloo* 6, no. 2 (spring–summer 1983): 74–83.

Clothier, Peter. *Betye Saar.* Los Angeles: Museum of Contemporary Art, 1984.

Cole, Joanna. *Best Loved Folktales.* New York: Anchor, 1983.

Collier, Eugenia. "The Closing of the Circle: Movement from Division to Wholeness in Paule Marshall's Fiction." In *Black Women Writers (1950–1980): A Critical Evaluation,* ed. Mari Evans, 295–315. New York: Doubleday, 1984.

Collins, Patricia Hill. *Black Feminist Thought: Knowledge, Consciousness, and the Politics of Empowerment.* New York: Routledge, 1990.

Combahee River Collective. "A Black Feminist Statement." In *All the Women Are White, All the Blacks Are Men, but Some of Us Are Brave: Black Women's Studies,* ed. Gloria T. Hull, Patricia Bell-Scott, and Barbara Smith, 13–22. Old Westbury, N.Y.: Feminist Press, 1982.

Conwill, Houston. "An Interview with Betye Saar." *Black Art: An International Quarterly* 1 (fall 1978): 4–14.

Coser, Stelamaris. *Bridging the Americas: The Literature of Paule Marshall, Toni Morrison, and Gayle Jones.* Philadelphia: Temple University Press, 1994.

Cruse, Harold. *The Crisis of the Negro Intellectual.* New York: William Morrow, 1967.

Damsker, Matt. "Performance Creates a Tableau." *Los Angeles Times,* February 17, 1984, 1–2.

Davies, Carole Boyce. *Black Women, Writing, and Identity: Migrations of the Subject.* London: Routledge, 1994.

————. "Mothering and Healing in Recent Black Women's Fiction." *Sage* 1 (spring 1985): 41–43.

Davis, Angela. "Reflections on the Black Woman's Role in the Community of Slaves." *The Black Scholar* 3, no. 4 (December 1971): 2–15.

Davis, Donn Granville. "Image • Symbol Control and the Black Arts: A Tentative Note on the Need for Organization." *Black Art: An International Quarterly* 3 (spring 1979): 32–36.

Demetrakopoulos, Stephanie. "Morrison's Creation of White World: *Tar Baby* and Irreconcilable Polarities." In *New Dimensions of Spirituality: A Biracial and Bicultural Reading of the Novels of Toni Morrison,* ed. Karla F. C. Holloway and Stephanie Demetrakopoulos, 131–42. New York: Greenwood Press, 1987.

Desmangles, Leslie. *The Faces of the Gods: Vodou and Roman Catholicism in Haiti.* Chapel Hill: University of North Carolina Press, 1992.

Diop, Cheik Anta. *The African Origin of Civilization: Myth or Reality.* Trans. Mercer Cook. Westport, Conn.: Lawrence Hill, 1974.

Dishman, Laura Stewart. "Ringgold Uses Fabric as a Thread to Her Past." *Orlando Sentinel,* September 11, 1987, E2.

Driskell, David. *Two Centuries of Black American Art*. Los Angeles: Los Angeles County Museum of Art; New York: Alfred A. Knopf, 1976.

Driskell, David, ed. *African American Visual Aesthetics: A Postmodernist View*. Washington: Smithsonian Institution Press, 1995.

Driver, Tom F. *Liberating Rites: Understanding the Transformative Power of Ritual*. Boulder, Colo.: Westview Press, 1998.

Dubey, Madhu. *Black Women Novelists and the Nationalist Aesthetic*. Bloomington: Indiana University Press, 1994.

Dundes, Alan. *Interpreting Folklore*. Bloomington: Indiana University Press, 1980.

Dundes, Alan, ed. *Mother Wit from the Laughing Barrel: Readings in the Interpretation of Afro-American Folklore*. Englewood Cliffs, N.J.: Prentice Hall, 1973.

————. *The Study of Folklore*. Englewood Cliffs, N.J.: Prentice Hall, 1965.

Ellison, Ralph. "Change the Joke and Slip the Yoke." In *Mother Wit from the Laughing Barrel: Readings in the Interpretation of Afro-American Folklore*, ed. Alan Dundes, 56–64. Englewood Cliffs, N.J.: Prentice Hall, 1973.

Epps, Archie, ed. *The Speeches of Malcolm X at Harvard*. New York: William Morrow, 1968.

Evans, Mari, ed. *Black Women Writers (1950–1980): A Critical Evaluation*. New York: Doubleday, 1984.

Fabio, Sarah Webster. "Tripping with Black Writing." In *The Black Aesthetic*, ed. Addison Gayle Jr., 173–81. New York: Anchor, 1971.

Faith Ringgold: A Twenty-five Year Survey: April 1 to June 24, 1990. Eleanor Flomenhaft, curator. Hempstead, N.Y.: Fine Arts Museum of Long Island, 1990.

Faith Ringgold—Change: Painted Story Quilts. New York: Bernice Steinbaum Gallery, 1987.

Faith Ringgold: Twenty Years of Painting, Sculpture, and Performance, 1963–1983. New York: Studio Museum in Harlem, 1984.

Ferris, William. *Afro-American Folk Art and Craft*. Jackson: University Press of Mississippi, 1983.

Fine, Elsa Honing. *The Afro-American Artist: A Search for Identity*. New York: Holt, Rinehart, and Winston, 1973.

Fowler, Carolyn. *Black Arts and Black Aesthetics*. Atlanta: First World Publishing, 1976.

———. "The Black Writer and His Role." In *The Black Aesthetic*, ed. Addison Gayle Jr., 349–56. New York: Anchor, 1971.

Fox, Catherine. "The Artist as Shaman: The Ordinary Becomes Special with Betye Saar." *Atlanta Journal-Constitution Weekend*, February 11, 1984, 5.

Fuller, Hoyt. "The New Black Literature: Protest or Affirmation." In *The Black Aesthetic*, ed. Addison Gayle Jr., 327–48. New York: Anchor, 1971.

Fusco, Coco. *English Is Broken Here: Notes on Cultural Fusion in the Americas*. New York: New Press, 1995.

Galligan, Gregory. "The Quilts of Faith Ringgold." *Arts* 61, no. 5 (January 1987): 62–63.

Gates, Henry Louis, Jr. *Figures in Black: Words, Signs, and the "Racial" Self*. New York: Oxford University Press, 1987.

———. "The Master's Pieces: On Canon Formation and the African American Tradition." *South Atlantic Quarterly* 89 (1990): 89–111.

Gates, Henry Louis, Jr., and K. A. Appiah, eds. *Toni Morrison: Critical Perspectives Past and Present*. New York: Amistad Press, 1993.

Gayle, Addison, Jr., ed. *The Black Aesthetic*. New York: Anchor, 1971.

———. *The Way of the New World*. New York: Doubleday, 1975.

Georges, Robert, and Michael Owen Jones. *Folkloristics: An Introduction*. Bloomington: Indiana University Press, 1995.

Gilroy, Paul. *The Black Atlantic: Modernity and Double Consciousness*. Cambridge: Harvard University Press, 1993.

———. "Roots and Routes: Black Identity as an Outernational Project." In *Racial and Ethnic Identity: Psychological Development and Creative Expression*, ed. Herbert W. Harris, Howard Blue, and E. H. Griffith, 15–30. New York: Routledge, 1995.

Giroux, Henry. *Border Crossings: Cultural Workers and the Politics of Education*. New York: Routledge, 1992.

Giroux, Henry, and Peter McLaren, eds. *Between Borders: Pedagogy and the Politics of Cultural Studies*. New York: Routledge, 1994.

Glueck, Grace. "Art: Betye Saar Gives Spirits Form." *New York Times*, April 18, 1980.

————. "An Artist Who Turns Cloth into Social Commentary." *New York Times*, July 29, 1984, 25.

————. "Betye Saar, Artist Inspired by the Occult." *New York Times*, February 16, 1978.

Goldwater, Robert. "The Western Experience of Negro Art." In *Colloquium on Negro Art: Publication of the First World Festival of Negro Arts, Dakar, April 1–24, 1966*, 337–50. Paris: Présence Africaine, 1968.

Gomez-Peña, Guillermo. *Warrior for Gringostroika: Essays, Performance, Texts, and Poetry*. St. Paul: Graywolf Press, 1993.

Gonzalez-Whippler, Migene. *Santeria: African Magic in Latin America*. New York: Julian Press, 1973.

————. *Santeria: The Religion, A Legacy of Faith, Rites, and Magic*. New York: Harmony Books, 1989.

Gouma-Peterson, Thalia. "Faith Ringgold's Narrative Quilts." In *Faith Ringgold—Change: Painted Story Quilts*, 9–16. New York: Bernice Steinbaum Gallery, 1987.

————. "Modern Dilemma Tales: Faith Ringgold's Story Quilts." In *Faith Ringgold: A Twenty-five Year Survey*. Hempstead, N.Y.: Fine Arts Museum of Long Island, 1990.

Grant, Joanne, ed. *Black Protest: History, Documents, and Analyses, 1619–Present*. New York: Fawcett Premier, 1991.

Hall, Michael, et al. *The Artist Outsider: Creativity and the Boundaries of Culture*. Washington: Smithsonian Institution Press, 1994.

Hall, Stuart. "Cultural Identity and Diaspora." In *Identity, Community, Culture, Difference*, ed. Jonathan Rutherford, 222–37. London: Lawrence and Wishart, 1990.

Halpin, Marjorie. "Confronting the Looking-Glass Men: A Preliminary Examination of the Mask." In *Ritual Symbolism and Ceremonialism in the Americas: Studies in Symbolic Anthropology*, vol. 1, ed. N. Ross Crumrine, 41–62. Greeley: University of Northern Colorado, 1979.

Hamilton, Virginia. *The People Could Fly: American Black Folktales*. New York: Alfred Knopf, 1985.

Hammond, Leslie King. *Ritual and Myth: A Survey of African American Art, June 20, 1982–November 1, 1982*. New York: Studio Museum in Harlem, 1982.

Harris, Joel Chandler. *The Favorite Uncle Remus*. New York: Houghton
    Mifflin, 1948.
Harris, Norman. *Connecting Times: The Sixties in Afro-American Fic-
    tion*. Jackson: University of Mississippi Press, 1988.
Harris, Trudier. *Exorcising Blackness: Historical and Literary Lynching
    and Burning Rituals*. Bloomington: Indiana University Press,
    1984.
———. *Fiction and Folklore: The Novels of Toni Morrison*. Knoxville:
    University of Tennessee Press, 1991.
Hartsock, Nancy. "Rethinking Modernism: Minority vs. Majority
    Theories." In *The Nature and Context of Minority Discourse*, ed.
    Abdul JanMohamed and David Lloyd, 17–36. New York: Ox-
    ford University Press, 1990.
Henderson, Mae G., ed. *Borders, Boundaries, and Frames: Essays in
    Cultural Criticism and Cultural Studies*. New York: Routledge,
    1995.
Henderson, Stephen. Introduction to *Black Women Writers (1950–
    1980): A Critical Evaluation*, ed. Mari Evans, xxiii–xxvii. Garden
    City, N.Y.: Anchor, 1984.
———. *Understanding the New Black Poetry*. New York: William Mor-
    row, 1973.
Henkes, Robert. *The Art of Black American Women: Works of Twenty-
    four Artists of the Twentieth Century*. Jefferson, N.C.: McFarland,
    1993.
Hernton, Calvin. *The Sexual Mountain and Black Women Writers*. New
    York: Doubleday, 1987.
Herron, Leonora, and Alice M. Bacon. "Conjuring and Conjure-
    Doctors." In *Mother Wit from the Laughing Barrel: Readings in the
    Interpretation of Afro-American Folklore*, ed. Alan Dundes, 359–
    68. Englewood Cliffs, N.J.: Prentice Hall, 1973.
Herskovits, Melville. *The Myth of the Negro Past*. Boston: Beacon Press,
    1958.
High-Wasikhongo, Frieda. "Afrofemcentric: Twenty Years of Faith
    Ringgold." In *Faith Ringgold: Twenty Years of Painting, Sculpture,
    and Performance, 1963–1983*, 17–18. New York: Studio Museum
    in Harlem, 1984.
Holloway, Karla F. C. "African Values and Western Chaos." In *New
    Dimensions of Spirituality: A Biracial and Bicultural Reading of the*

Novels of Toni Morrison, ed. Karla F. C. Holloway and Stephanie Demetrakopoulos, 117–29. New York: Greenwood Press, 1987.

———. "On Morrison and Black Female Memory." In *New Dimensions of Spirituality: A Biracial and Bicultural Reading of the Novels of Toni Morrison*, ed. Karla F. C. Holloway and Stephanie Demetrakopoulos, 149–56. New York: Greenwood Press, 1987.

Holloway, Karla F. C., and Stephanie Demetrakopoulos, eds. *New Dimensions of Spirituality: A Biracial and Bicultural Reading of the Novels of Toni Morrison*. New York: Greenwood Press, 1987.

hooks, bell. *Art on My Mind: Visual Politics*. New York: New Press, 1995.

———. *Black Looks: Race and Representation*. Boston: South End Press, 1992.

———. *Yearning: Race, Gender, and Cultural Politics*. Boston: South End Press, 1990.

Hughes, Langston, and Arna Bontemps, eds. *The Book of Negro Folklore*. New York: Dodd, Mead, 1958.

Hull, Gloria T., Patricia Bell-Scott, and Barbara Smith. *All the Women Are White, All the Blacks Are Men, but Some of Us Are Brave: Black Women's Studies*. Old Westbury, N.Y.: Feminist Press, 1982.

Hurston, Zora Neale. *Mules and Men*. 1935. Reprint, Bloomington: Indiana University Press, 1978.

———. *The Sanctified Church: Folklore Writings of Zora Neale Hurston*. Berkeley: Turtle Island Foundation, 1981.

———. *Tell My Horse: Voodoo and Life in Haiti and Jamaica*. 1938. Reprint, New York: Harper and Row, 1990.

Hyatt, Harry M., ed. *Hoodoo-Conjuration-Witchcraft, and Rootwork*. 5 vols. Washington: American University Bookstore, 1970.

Hyman, Jacques Louis. *Leopold Sedar Senghor: An Intellectual Biography*. Chicago: Aldine-Atherton, 1971.

Hyman, Stanley Edgar. "The Folk Tradition." In *Mother Wit from the Laughing Barrel: Readings in the Interpretation of Afro-American Folklore*, ed. Alan Dundes, 45–56. Englewood Cliffs, N.J.: Prentice Hall, 1973.

Irele, Abiola. *The African Experience in Literature and Ideology*. Bloomington: Indiana University Press, 1990.

———. "Négritude or Black Cultural Nationalism." *Journal of Modern African Studies* 3 (1965): 321–71.

Jahn, Janheinz. *Muntu: An Outline of New African Culture*. Trans. Marjorie Grene. New York: Grove Press, 1961.

———. *Neo-African Literature*. New York: Grove Press, 1969.

James, Michael. "Beyond the Tradition: The Art of the Studio Quilt." *American Craft*, February–March 1985, 17–22.

James, Stanlie, and Abena Busia, eds. *Theorizing Black Feminisms*. New Haven: Yale University Press, 1994.

Jameson, Fredric. *The Political Unconscious: Narrative as a Socially Symbolic Act*. Ithaca: Cornell University Press, 1981.

JanMohamed, Abdul, and David Lloyd, eds. *The Nature and Context of Minority Discourse*. New York: Oxford University Press, 1990.

Jarrell, Wadsworth A. "Heading for a Black Aesthetic." *Art Papers* 6 (1985): 16–19.

Johnson, Barbara. *A World of Difference*. Baltimore: Johns Hopkins University Press, 1987.

Johnson, Charles. *Being and Race: Black Writing since 1970*. Bloomington: Indiana University Press, 1988.

Jones, LeRoi [Amiri Baraka]. *Blues People: The Negro Experience in White America and the Music that Developed from It*. New York: William Morrow, 1963.

———. "The Changing Same (R&B and New Black Music)." In *The Black Aesthetic*, ed. Addison Gayle Jr., 112–25. New York: Anchor, 1971.

Jones, LeRoi, and Larry Neal, eds. *Black Fire: An Anthology of Afro-American Writing*. New York: William Morrow, 1968.

Karenga, Ron [Maulana]. "Black Cultural Nationalism." In *The Black Aesthetic*, ed. Addison Gayle Jr., 31–37. New York: Anchor, 1971.

Kramer, Victor, ed. *The Harlem Renaissance Re-examined*. New York: AMS Press, 1987.

La Duke, Betty. *Africa through the Eyes of Women Artists*. Trenton, N.J.: Africa World Press, 1991.

Le Clair, Thomas. "A Conversation with Toni Morrison: 'The Language Must Not Sweat.'" *New Republic*, March 21, 1981, 25–32.

Levine, Lawrence. *Black Culture and Black Consciousness: Afro-American Folk Thought from Slavery to Freedom*. New York: Oxford University Press, 1977.

Lindsay, Arturo, ed. *Santeria Aesthetics in Contemporary Latin American Art*. Washington: Smithsonian Institution Press, 1996.

Lionnet, Françoise. *Postcolonial Representations: Women, Literature, Identity.* Ithaca: Cornell University Press, 1995.

Lippard, Lucy. *Mixed Blessings: New Art in a Multicultural America.* New York: Pantheon, 1990.

Liss, Andrea. "Power and Gentle Force." *Artweek,* February 27, 1988, 3.

Locke, Alain. *Negro Art: Past and Present.* Washington: Associates in Negro Folk Education, 1936.

Locke, Alain, ed. *The New Negro.* 1925. Reprint, New York: Atheneum, 1992.

Long, Richard A., and Eugenia Collier, eds. *Afro-American Writing: An Anthology.* University Park: Pennsylvania State University Press, 1985.

Lorde, Audre. "Learning from the Sixties." In *Sister Outsider: Essays and Speeches,* 134–44. Trumansburg, N.Y.: Crossing Press, 1984.

Lornell, Kip. *"Happy in the Service of the Lord": African American Sacred Vocal Harmony Quartets in Memphis.* Knoxville: University of Tennessee Press, 1995.

Lott, Eric. *Love and Theft: Blackface Minstrelsy and the American Working Class.* New York: Oxford University Press, 1993.

Malinowski, Bronislaw. *Magic, Science, Religion, and Other Essays.* New York: Doubleday, 1954.

Marcus, Harriett P. "Once More with Feeling: The Art of Betye Saar." *Park Forest (Ill.) Star,* February 1979, 25.

Markovitz, Irving Leonard. *Leopold Sedar Senghor and the Politics of Négritude.* New York: Atheneum, 1969.

Marshall, Paule. *Brown Girl, Brownstones.* New York: Random House, 1959.

———. *The Chosen Place, the Timeless People.* New York: Harcourt, Brace and World, 1969. Reprint, New York: Vintage, 1984.

———. "From the Poet's Kitchen." *Callaloo* 6, no. 2 (1983): 23–29.

———. "The Negro Woman in American Literature." *Freedomways* 1 (1966): 8–24.

———. *Praisesong for the Widow.* New York: G. Putnam's Sons, 1983. Reprint, New York: E. P. Dutton, 1984.

———. "Shaping the World of My Art." *New Letters* 1 (1973): 97–112.

Mazrui, Ali A. *Cultural Forces in World Politics.* Portsmouth, N.H.: Heinemann Educational Books, 1990.

Mbiti, John. *Concepts of God in Africa*. New York: Praeger Publishers, 1970.

McCall, George. "Symbiosis: The Case of Hoodoo and the Numbers Racket." In *Mother Wit from the Laughing Barrel: Readings in the Interpretation of Afro-American Folklore*, ed. Alan Dundes, 419–27. Englewood Cliffs, N.J.: Prentice Hall, 1973.

McDowell, Deborah. "The 'Changing Same': Generational Connections and Black Women Novelists." *New Literary History* 2 (winter 1987): 280–302.

———. "New Directions for Black Feminist Criticism." In *New Feminist Criticism*, ed. Elaine Showalter, 186–97. New York: Pantheon, 1985.

McKay, Nellie, ed. *Critical Essays on Toni Morrison*. Boston: G. K. Hall, 1988.

Miller, Lynn F., and Sally Swenson. "Betye Saar." In *Lives and Works: Talks with Women Artists*. Metuchen, N.J.: Scarecrow Press, 1981.

———. "Faith Ringgold." In *Lives and Works: Talks with Women Artists*. Metuchen, N.J.: Scarecrow Press, 1981.

Minh-ha, Trinh T. *Woman, Native, Other: Writing Postcoloniality and Feminism*. Bloomington: Indiana University Press, 1989.

Mitchell, Henry. *Black Belief: Folk Beliefs of Blacks in America and West Africa*. New York: Harper and Row, 1975.

Mol, Hans. *Identity and the Sacred*. New York: Free Press, 1976.

Morrison, Toni. *The Bluest Eye*. New York: Holt, Rinehart and Winston, 1970.

———. "City Limits, Village Values: Concepts of Neighborhood in Black Fiction." In *Literature and the Urban Experience: Essays on the City and Literature*, ed. Michael C. Jaye and Anne Watts, 35–43. New Brunswick: Rutgers University Press, 1981.

———. "Rediscovering Black History." *New York Times Magazine*, August 11, 1974, 14–24.

———. "Rootedness: The Ancestor as Foundation." In *Black Women Writers (1950–1980): A Critical Evaluation*, ed. Mari Evans, 339–45. New York: Anchor, 1984.

———. "A Slow Walk of Trees (as Grandmother Would Say) Hopeless (as Grandfather Would Say)." *New York Times Magazine*, July 4, 1976.

———. *Song of Solomon*. New York: Alfred Knopf, 1977.

————. *Sula*. New York: Alfred Knopf, 1973.

————. *Tar Baby*. New York: Alfred Knopf, 1981.

Munro, Eleanor. "Betye Saar." In *Originals, American Women Artists*. New York: Simon and Schuster, 1979.

————. "Faith Ringgold." In *Originals, American Women Artists*. New York: Simon and Schuster, 1979.

————. "Who's Afraid of Aunt Jemima?: History and Style." In *Faith Ringgold: Twenty Years of Painting, Sculpture, and Performance, 1963–1983*, 21. New York: Studio Museum in Harlem, 1984.

Murray, Pauli. "Jim Crow and Jane Crow." In *Black Women in White America*, ed. Gerda Lerner, 592–99. New York: Random House, 1973.

Naylor, Gloria. " 'A Conversation': Toni Morrison and Gloria Naylor." *The Southern Review* 3 (1985): 567–93.

Neal, Larry. "The Black Arts Movement." In *The Black Aesthetic*, ed. Addison Gayle Jr., 256–74. New York: Anchor, 1971.

————. "Some Reflections on the Black Aesthetic." In *The Black Aesthetic*, ed. Addison Gayle Jr., 12–15. New York: Anchor, 1971.

O'Meally, Robert J. " 'Tar Baby, She Don't Say Nothin'.' " *Callaloo 11–13*, 4 (1981): 193–97.

Oring, Elliott, ed. *Folk Groups and Folklore Genres: A Reader*. Logan: Utah State University Press, 1989.

Parker, Bettye J. "Complexity: Toni Morrison's Women—An Interview Essay." In *Sturdy Black Bridges: Visions of Black Women in Literature*, ed. Roseann P. Bell, et al., 251–57. Garden City, N.Y.: Anchor, 1979.

Parsons, Elsie Clews. *Folklore of the Antilles, French and English*. New York: American Folklore Society, 1943.

Perry, Ruth, and Martine Watson Brownley. *Mothering the Mind: Twelve Stories of Writers and Their Silent Partners*. New York: Holmes and Meier, 1984.

Pettis, Joyce. *Toward Wholeness in Paule Marshall's Fiction*. Charlottesville: University Press of Virginia, 1995.

Pettit, Susan. "Saar Explores Interior Space." *A Museum of Contemporary Art Publication* 1, no. 3 (summer 1984): 7.

Phelan, Peggy. *Unmarked: The Politics of Performance*. New York: Routledge, 1993.

Picton, John, and John Mack. *African Textiles*. London: British Museum Publications, 1989.

Porter, James. *Modern Negro Art*. New York: Dryden Press, 1943.

Powell, Richard. *Black Art and Culture in the Twentieth Century*. London: Thames of Hudson, 1997.

Price, Sally, and Richard Price. *Afro-American Arts of the Suriname Rain Forest*. Berkeley and Los Angeles: University of California Press, 1980.

Pryse, Marjorie. "Zora Neale Hurston, Alice Walker, and the 'Ancient Power' of Black Women." In *Conjuring: Black Women, Fiction, and Literary Tradition*, ed. Marjorie Pryse and Hortense Spillers, 1–24. Bloomington: Indiana University Press, 1985.

Puckett, Newbell Niles. *Folk Beliefs of the Southern Negro*. Chapel Hill: University of North Carolina Press, 1926.

Ransaw, Lee. "The Changing Relationship of the Black Visual Artist to His Community." *Black Art: An International Quarterly* 2 (1979): 44–56.

Reed, Ishmael. "Can a Metronome Know the Thunder or Summon a God?" In *The Black Aesthetic*, ed. Addison Gayle Jr., 381–82. New York: Anchor, 1971.

Reyes, Angelita. "Ancient Properties of the New World: The Paradox of the 'Other' in Toni Morrison's *Tar Baby*." *The Black Scholar* 2 (March/April 1986): 19–25.

Ringgold, Faith. *We Flew over the Bridge: The Memoirs of Faith Ringgold*. Boston: Little, Brown, 1995.

———. "Who's Afraid of Aunt Jemima?: A Book of Story Quilts and Personal Narrative on the Life of Faith Ringgold." Courtesy Bernice Steinbaum Gallery, N.Y. Typescript.

———. "Women's Traditional Art." *Heresies: A Feminist Publication on Art and Politics* 1 (winter 1977–1978): 84.

Ritual and Myth: A Survey of African American Art, June 20, 1982– November 1, 1982. New York: Studio Museum in Harlem, 1982.

Rituals: The Art of Betye Saar. New York: Studio Museum in Harlem, 1980.

Rosenberg, Bruce. *Folklore and Literature: Rival Siblings*. Knoxville: University of Tennessee Press, 1991.

Rosing, Larry. "Betye Saar." *Arts Magazine: Ideas in Contemporary Art* 10 (1976): 7.

Rouse, Terrie. "Faith Ringgold—A Mirror of Her Community." In *Faith Ringgold: Twenty Years of Painting, Sculpture, and Performance, 1963–1983*, 9–10. New York: Studio Museum in Harlem, 1984.

Rubin, Arnold. "Accumulation: Power and Display in African Sculpture." *Artforum* (May 1975): 35–47.

Rutherford, Jonathan. *Identity: Community, Culture, Difference.* London: Lawrence and Wishart, 1990.

Saar, Betye. "Installation as Sculpture." *International Review of African American Art* 1 (1984): 44–48.

Savannah Unit of the Georgia Writers Project. *Drums and Shadows: Survival Studies among the Georgia Coastal Negroes.* Athens: University of Georgia Press, 1940. Reprint, Athens: Brown Thrasher, 1986.

Schechner, Richard. *The Future of Ritual: Writings on Culture and Performance.* London: Routledge, 1993.

Segy, Ladislas. *Masks of Black Africa.* New York: Dover, 1976.

Senghor, Leopold. *The Foundations of "Africanité," or "Négritude" and "Arabité."* Trans. Mercer Cook. Paris: Presence Africaine, 1971.

———. "Négritude: A Humanism of the Twentieth Century." In *The African Reader: Independent Africa,* ed. Wilfred Cartey and Martin Kilson, 179–92. New York: Random House, 1970.

Singh, Amritjit, Joseph T. Skerrett Jr., and Robert Hogan, eds. *Memory, Narrative, and Identity.* Boston: Northeastern University Press, 1994.

Smith, Theophus H. *Conjuring Culture: Biblical Formations of Black America.* New York: Oxford University Press, 1994.

Sollors, Werner, and Maria Diedrich, eds. *The Black Columbiad: Defining Moments in African American Literature and Culture.* Cambridge: Harvard University Press, 1994.

Steigerwald, David. *The Sixties and the End of Modern America.* New York: St. Martin's Press, 1994.

Stepto, Robert B. " 'Intimate Things in Place': An Interview with Toni Morrison." *Massachusetts Review* 3 (1977): 474–89.

Stoelting, Winifred L. "Time Past and Time Present: The Search for Viable Links in *The Chosen Place, The Timeless People* by Paule Marshall." *CLA Journal* 1 (1972): 60–71.

Strouse, Jean. "Toni Morrison's Black Magic." *Newsweek*, March 30, 1981, 52–57.

Stuckey, Sterling. "Through the Prism of Folklore." *Massachusetts Review* 9 (1968): 417–37.

Tate, Claudia, ed. *Black Women Writers at Work*. New York: Continuum, 1983.

———. *Psychoanalysis and Black Novels: Desire and the Protocols of Race*. New York: Oxford University Press, 1998.

Taylor-Guthrie, Danille, ed. *Conversations with Toni Morrison*. Jackson: University Press of Mississippi, 1994.

Thompson, Robert Farris. *African Art in Motion*. Berkeley and Los Angeles: University of California Press, 1974.

———. *Flash of the Spirit: African and Afro-American Art and Philosophy*. New York: Vintage, 1984.

Tradition and Conflict: Images of a Turbulent Decade, 1963–1973. New York: Studio Museum in Harlem, 1985.

Turner, Patricia. *Ceramic Uncles and Celluloid Mammies: Black Images and Their Influence on Culture*. New York: Anchor, 1994.

Turner, Victor. *The Ritual Process: Structure and Anti-structure*. Ithaca: Cornell University Press, 1969.

Vlach, John. *The Afro-American Tradition in the Decorative Arts*. Athens: University of Georgia Press, 1990.

Wade-Gayles, Gloria. *No Crystal Stair: Visions of Race and Gender in Black Women's Fiction*. Rev. ed. Cleveland: Pilgrim Press, 1997.

Wahlman, Maude. *Contemporary African Arts*. Chicago: Field Museum of Natural History, 1974.

———. "Religious Symbolism in African-American Quilts." *The Clarion* (summer 1989): 36–44.

Walker, Sheila. *Ceremonial Spirit Possession in Africa and Afro-America: Forms, Meanings, and Functional Significance for Individuals and Social Groups*. Leiden: E. J. Brill, 1972.

Wall, Cheryl, ed. *Changing Our Own Words: Essays on Criticism and Writing by Black Women*. New Brunswick: Rutgers University Press, 1989.

Wallace, Michele. *Invisibility Blues: From Pop to Theory*. London: Verso, 1990.

———. "Modernism, Postmodernism, and the Problem of the Visual in Afro-American Culture." In *Aesthetics in Feminist Perspective*, ed. Hilde Hein and Carolyn Korsmeyer, 205–17. Bloomington: Indiana University Press, 1993.

Washington, Mary Helen. "I Sign My Mother's Name: Alice Walker, Dorothy West, Paule Marshall." In *Writing Lives: Conversations between Women Writers*, ed. Mary Chamberlain. London: Virago Press, 1988. [This essay originally appeared, in slightly different form, in *Mothering the Mind: Twelve Studies of Writers and Their Silent Partners*, ed. Ruth Perry and Marture Watson Brownley. New York: Holmes and Meier, 1984.]

Washington, Mary Helen, ed. *Midnight Birds: Stories of Contemporary Black Women Writers*. Garden City, N.Y.: Anchor, 1980.

Wellburn, Ron. "The Black Aesthetic Imperative." In *The Black Aesthetic*, ed. Addison Gayle Jr., 126–42. New York: Anchor, 1971.

Whitten, Norman. "Contemporary Patterns of Malign Occultism." In *Mother Wit from the Laughing Barrel: Readings in the Interpretation of Afro-American Folklore*, ed. Alan Dundes, 402–18. Englewood Cliffs, N.J.: Prentice Hall, 1973.

Williams, John, trans. "Return of a Native Daughter: An Interview with Paule Marshall and Maryse Conde." *Sage* 2 (1986): 52–53.

Williams-Jones, Pearl. "Performance Style in Black Gospel Music." In *Black People and Their Culture*, ed. Linn Shapiro, 115–19. Washington: Smithsonian Institution, 1976.

Willis, Deborah. *Picturing Us: African American Identity in Photography*. New York: New Press, 1994.

Willis, Susan. "Black Women Writers: Taking a Critical Perspective." In *Making A Difference: Feminist Literary Criticism*, 211–37. New York: Methuen, 1985.

———. "Eruptions of Funk: Historicizing Toni Morrison." In *Black Literature and Literary Theory*, ed. Henry Louis Gates Jr., 263–83. New York: Methuen, 1984.

Winsbro, Bonnie. *Supernatural Forces: Belief, Difference, and Power in Contemporary Works by Ethnic Women*. Amherst: University of Massachusetts Press, 1993.

With Fingers of Love: Economic Development and the Civil Rights Movement. 27 min. Princeton, N.J.: Films for the Humanities and Sciences, 1995. Videocassette.

Yawney, Carole D. "Dread Wasteland: Rastafarian Ritual." In *Ritual Symbolism and Ceremonialism in the Americas: Studies in Symbolic*

Anthropology, vol. 1, ed. N. Ross Crumrine, 154–78. Greeley: University of Northern Colorado, 1979.

Zahan, Dominique. *The Religion, Spirituality, and Thought of Traditional Africa.* Chicago: University of Chicago Press, 1979.

Index